Due	Return	Due	Return
Date	Date	Date	Date

AN ESSAY

ON

FREDERIC THE GREAT.

AMS PRESS

NEW YORK

ENGLISH CLASSIC SERIES.— Nos. 108-109.

AN ESSAY

ON

FREDERIC THE GREAT.

BY

THOMAS BABINGTON MACAULAY.

WITH BIOGRAPHICAL SKETCH OF MACAULAY

AND WITH

Explanatory and Biographical Notes.

1893

NEW YORK:

MAYNARD, MERRILL, & CO.,

43, 45 and 47 East Tenth Street

Library of Congress Cataloging in Publication Data

Macaulay, Thomas Babington Macaulay, Baron, 1800-1859.
    An essay on Frederic the Great.

    Originally published in 1878 under title: Frederic
the Great.
    Reprint of the ed. published by Maynard, Merrill,
New York, which was issued as no. 108-109 of English
classic series.
    1. Friedrich II, der Grosse, King of Prussia, 1712-1786
I. Title.
DD404.M2   1975   943'.053'0924 [B]   73-137257
ISBN 0-404-04100-0

From the edition of 1893, New York
First AMS edition published in 1975
Manufactured in the United States of America

AMS PRESS INC.
NEW YORK, N. Y. 10003

LIFE OF MACAULAY.

THOMAS BABINGTON MACAULAY, whose father was Zachary Macaulay—famous for his advocacy of the abolition of slavery, was born at Rothley Temple, in Leicestershire, towards the end of 1800. From his infancy he showed a precocity that was simply extraordinary. He not only acquired knowledge rapidly, but he possessed a marvelous power of working it up into literary form, and his facile pen produced compositions in prose and in verse, histories, odes, and hymns. From the time that he was three years old he read incessantly, for the most part lying on the rug before the fire with his book on the ground, and a piece of bread and butter in his hand. It is told of him that when a boy of four, and on a visit with his father, he was unfortunate enough to have a cup of hot coffee overturned on his legs, and when his hostess, in her sympathetic kindness, asked shortly after how he was feeling, he looked up in her face and said, "Thank you, madam, the agony is abated." At seven he wrote a compendium of Universal History. At eight he was so fired with the *Lay* and with *Marmion* that he wrote three cantos of a poem in imitation of Scott's manner, and called it the "Battle of Cheviot." And he had many other literary projects, in all of which he showed perfect correctness both in grammar and in spelling, made his meaning uniformly clear, and was scrupulously accurate in his punctuation.

With all this cleverness he was not conceited. His parents, and particularly his mother, were most judicious in their treatment. They never encouraged him to display his powers of conversation, and they abstained from every kind of remark that might help him to think himself different from other boys. One result was that throughout his life he was free from literary vanity; another was that he habitually overestimated the knowledge of others. When he said in his essays that every schoolboy knew

3

this and that fact in history, he was judging their information by his own vast intellectual stores.

At the age of twelve, Macaulay was sent to a private school in the neighborhood of Cambridge. There he laid the foundation of his future scholarship, and though fully occupied with his school work—chiefly Latin, Greek, and mathematics—he found time to gratify his insatiable thirst for general literature. He read at random and without restraint, but with an apparent partiality for the lighter and more attractive books. Poetry and prose fiction remained throughout his life his favorite reading. On subjects of this nature he displayed a most unerring memory, as well as the capacity for taking in at a glance the contents of a printed page. Whatever caught his fancy he remembered, as well as though he had consciously got it by heart. He once said, that if all the copies of *Paradise Lost* and the *Pilgrim's Progress* were to be destroyed, he would from memory alone undertake to reproduce both.

In 1818 Macaulay went from school to the university—to Trinity College, Cambridge. But here the studies were not to his mind. He had no liking for mathematics, and was nowhere as a mathematical student. His inclination was wholly for literature, and he gained various high distinctions in that department. It was unfortunate for him that he had no severe discipline in scientific method ; to his disproportionate partiality for the lighter sides of literature must be attributed his want of philosophic grasp, his dislike to arduous speculations, and his want of courage in facing intellectual problems.

The private life of Cambridge had a much greater influence on him than the recognized studies of the place. He made many friends. His social qualities and his conversational powers were widely exercised and largely developed. He became, too, a brilliant member of the Union Debating Society, and here politics claimed his attention. Altogether he gave himself more to the enjoyment of all that was stirring around him than to the taking of university honors. In 1824, however, he was elected a Fellow, and began to take pupils. Further, he sought a wider field for his literary labors, and contributed papers to some of the magazines—mostly to *Knight's Quarterly Magazine.* Chief among these contributions are "Ivry," and "Naseby" in spirited verse, and the conversation between Cowley and Milton, in as splendid prose.

When Macaulay went to Cambridge, his father seemed in affluent circumstances, but the slave-trade agitation engrossed his time and his energy, and by and by there came on the family commercial ruin. This was a blow to the eldest son, but he bore up bravely, brought sunshine and happiness into the depressed household, and proceeded to retrieve their position with stern fortitude. He ultimately paid off his father's debts.

Though called to the bar in 1826, he did not take kindly to the law, and soon renounced it for an employment more congenial— literature. Already in 1824 he had been invited to write for the *Edinburgh Review,* and in August, 1825, appeared in that magazine his article on Milton, which created a sensation, and made the critics aware of the advent of a new literary power. This first success he followed up rapidly, and besides giving new life to the periodical, he soon gained for himself a name of note. In 1828 he was made a Commissioner of Bankruptcy, and in 1830 was elected M.P. for Calne. In the Reformed Parliament he sat for Leeds.

He entered Parliament at an opportune period, and was in the thick of the great Reform conflict. His speeches on the Reform Bill raised him to the first rank as an orator, and gained for him official posts. It was while burdened with these severe public labors that he wrote thirteen (from Montgomery to Pitt) of the *Edinburgh Review* Essays. Thus he went on for four years, but the narrow circumstances of his family induced him to accept the lucrative post of legal adviser to the Supreme Council of India. This necessitated his going to India, which was clearly adverse to his prospects at home; yet the certainty of returning with £20,000 saved from his large salary was sufficient inducement to make the sacrifice, and he sailed February 15, 1834.

In India he maintained his reputation as a hard worker. Besides his official duties as a Member of Council, he undertook the additional burden of acting as chairman in two important committees, and it is in connection with one of these—the committee appointed to draw up the new codes—that he has his chief title to fame as an Indian statesmen. The New Penal Code was in great part his work, and proves his wide acquaintance with English Criminal Law. He also took great part in the work of the Committee of Public Instruction, and was chiefly instrumental in introducing English studies among the native population. But he was not popular in Calcutta. Certain changes he helped to introduce roused the feeling of the English residents against him, and he was attacked in the most scurrilous way.

In 1838 he was back in England. Meanwhile he had written two more essays for the *Edinburgh*, one on Mackintosh and one on Bacon, and he was hardly home when there appeared another, that on Sir W. Temple. After spending the winter in Italy, he reviewed in 1839 Mr. Gladstone's book on *Church and State*, and might have settled down to purely literary life, but once more he was drawn into politics. Elected as Member for Edinburgh, he was soon admitted into the Cabinet as Secretary-at-War to the Whig Ministry of Lord Melbourne. The position, however, was no gain to Macaulay. He purposed to write "*A History of England*, from the accession of King James II., down to a time which is within the memory of men still living," and his official duties forced him to lay this project aside for the present.

Fortunately Lord Melbourne's ministry did not last long; it fell in 1841, and Macaulay was released from office. Still retaining his seat for Edinburgh, and speaking occasionally in the House he was free to follow his natural bent.

His leisure hours were given as usual to essay-work for the *Edinburgh*, and he wrote in succession Clive, Hastings, Frederick the Great, Addison, Chatham, etc. But in 1844 his connection with the *Review* came to an end, and he wrote no more for the Blue and Yellow, as it was called. In 1841 he had put forth a volume of poems—the *Lays of Ancient Rome*—not without misgivings as to the result. But the fresh and vigorous language at once carried the volume into popularity, and it had an enormous sale.

On a change of government in 1846, Macaulay, at the request of Lord John Russell, again became a Cabinet Minister, this time as Paymaster-General of the Army, and having to seek re-election from his constituents, went down to Scotland for the purpose. After a severe contest, and notwithstanding a growing unpopularity, he was successful. But at the general election of the following year the forces in opposition to him redoubled their energy, and he was defeated.

This was the real end of his political life. Although pressed to contest other seats, he resolutely declined, and for the next few years worked 'doggedly' at his *History*. In 1848 appeared the first two volumes, which had an immense success, 13,000 copies being sold in less than four months. The same year he was elected Lord Rector of Glasgow University. By 1852 the people of Edinburgh had repented the rejection of their famous Member, and took steps to re-elect him free of expense ; and so thoroughly was the scheme carried out that Macaulay, without having made a single speech, and without having visited the city, was returned triumphantly at the top of the poll. Through the length and breadth of the land the news was hailed with satisfaction, as an act of justice for an undeserved slight in the past. The result was very flattering to Macaulay, but he never really returned to political life as in his younger days. Moreover, forty years of incessant intellectual labors had begun to undermine his health, and he was now unequal to the fatigues that formerly were a pleasure to him. Accordingly in 1856, after having brought out the third and fourth volumes of his history, of which in a few months 25,000 copies were sold, he resigned his seat, and yielding too late obedience to all interested in his welfare, gave himself up to the enjoyment of that ease which he had faithfully earned. Then in 1857 he was created a Peer—Baron Macaulay of Rothley, his birthplace. Still struggling on with his *History* in the intermissions of his malady, he died suddenly on December 28, 1859. He was only fifty-nine—the victim of an appetite for work, insatiable and unfortunately too long ungoverned.

CRITICISM OF MACAULAY.

There is little to notice in Macaulay's vocabulary except its copiousness. He has no eccentricities like De Quincey or Carlyle; he employs neither slang nor scholastic technicalities, and he never coins a new word. He cannot be said to use an excess of Latin words, and he is not a purist in the matter of Saxon. His command of expression was proportioned to the extraordinary compass of his memory. The copiousness appears not so much in the Shakespearean form of accumulating synonyms one upon another as in a profuse way of repeating a thought in several different sentences. This is especially noticeable in the opening passages of some of his essays.

Macaulay's is a style that may truly be called "artificial" from his excessive use of striking artifices of style—balanced sentences, abrupt transitions, and pointed figures of speech. The peculiarities of the mechanism of his style are expressed in such general terms as "abrupt," "pointed," "oratorical." His sentences have the compact finish produced by the frequent occurrence of the periodic arrangement. He is not uniformly periodic; he often prefers a loose structure, and he very rarely has recourse to the forced inversions that we find occasionally in De Quincey. Yet there is a sufficient interspersion of periodic arrangements to produce an impression of firmness. . . .

Macaulay's composition is as far from being abstruse as printed matter can well be. One can trace in his writing a constant effort to make himself intelligible to the meanest capacity. He loves to dazzle and to argue, but above everything else he is anxious to be understood. His ideal evidently is to turn a subject over on every side, to place it in all lights, and to address himself to every variety of prejudice and preoccupation in his audience."— *William Minto.*

8

FREDERIC THE GREAT.

Frederic the Great and his Times. Edited, with an Introduction,
by THOMAS CAMPBELL, Esq. 2 vols., 8vo. London, 1842.

THIS work, which has the high honor of being introduced to
the world by the author of Lochiel and Hohenlinden, is not
wholly unworthy of so distinguished a *chaperon.* It pro-
fesses, indeed, to be no more than a compilation ; but it is an
exceedingly amusing compilation, and we shall be glad to 5
have more of it. The narrative comes down at present only
to the commencement of the Seven Years' War, and therefore
does not comprise the most interesting portion of Frederic's
reign.

It may not be unacceptable to our readers that we should 10
take this opportunity of presenting them with a slight sketch
of the life of the greatest king that has, in modern times, succeeded by right of birth to a throne. It may, we fear, be
impossible to compress so long and eventful a story within the
limits which we must prescribe to ourselves. Should we be 15
compelled to break off, we may perhaps, when the continua-
tion of this work appears, return to the subject.

---

7. **Seven Years' War.** The war of Frederic the Great of Prussia,
assisted by England, against Austria, Saxony, Russia, France, and Sweden.
The war lasted from 1756-1763,

The Prussian monarchy, the youngest of the great European
states, but in population and revenue the fifth among them,
and in art, science, and civilization entitled to the third, if
not to the second place, sprang from a humble origin. About
5 the beginning of the fifteenth century, the marquisate of
Brandenburg was bestowed by the Emperor Sigismund on the
noble family of Hohenzollern. In the sixteenth century that
family embraced the Lutheran doctrines. It obtained from
the King of Poland, early in the seventeenth century, the
10 investiture of the duchy of Prussia. Even after this accession
of territory, the chiefs of the House of Hohenzollern hardly
ranked with the Electors of Saxony and Bavaria. The soil of
Brandenburg was for the most part sterile. Even round
Berlin, the capital of the province, and round Potsdam, the
15 favorite residence of the Margraves, the country was a
desert. In some places, the deep sand could with difficulty be
forced by assiduous tillage to yield thin crops of rye and oats.
In other places, the ancient forests, from which the conquerors of the Roman empire had descended on the Danube,
20 remained untouched by the hand of man. Where the soil was
rich it was generally marshy, and its insalubrity repelled the
cultivators whom its fertility attracted. Frederic William,

---

7. **Hohenzollern.** In 1410, Sigismund was elected Emperor of Germany,
with the intriguing help of Frederic, Burggrave of Nuremberg. The next
year Sigismund invested Frederic with the marquisate of Brandenburg, as
a reward for his share in the imperial election.

The present Emperor of Germany is a member of the Hohenzollern
family, as was his grandfather William, who, with the help of Prince Bis-
marck, united the numerous petty kingdoms, principalities, and duchies of
Germany into one great Empire in 1871.

8. **Lutheran Doctrines.** Lutheranism is the prevailing form of Prot-
estantism in Germany. There are Lutheran churches in Russia, Holland,
France, Denmark, Norway, Sweden, and the United States. The Reformers
of the 16th century were called Lutherans by their adversaries. The name
was afterwards distinctively applied among Protestants to those who took
part with Martin Luther, particularly in the controversies regarding the
Lord's Supper.

12. **Electors.** In the 13th century the right of election of the German
Emperor, for a time exercised by all the German princes, was limited to
the holders of the highest offices in Church and State. Thus there came
to be seven electors—the electors of Mainz, Treves, and Cologne (ecclesiastical), and the Palatinate, Brandenburg, Saxony, and Bohemia. Later Bavaria
and Hanover became electorates.

15. **Margraves.** The Hohenzollern family. The title Margrave is equivalent to the English marquis. It is derived from Mark (border) and Graf
(count), and meant originally a keeper of the borders.

called the Great Elector, was the prince to whose policy his
successors have agreed to ascribe their greatness. He acquired by the peace of Westphalia several valuable possessions, and among them the rich city and district of Magdeburg ; and he left to his son Frederic a principality as con- 5
siderable as any which was not called a kingdom.

Frederic aspired to the style of royalty. Ostentatious and
profuse, negligent of his true interests and of his high duties,
insatiably eager for frivolous distinctions, he added nothing
to the real weight of the state which he governed : perhaps he 10
transmitted his inheritance to his children impaired rather
than augmented in value ; but he succeeded in gaining the
great object of his life, the title of King. In the year 1700 he
assumed this new dignity. He had on that occasion to under-
go all the mortifications which fall to the lot of ambitious 15
upstarts. Compared with the other crowned heads of Europe,
he made a figure resembling that which a Nabob or a Com-
missary, who had bought a title, would make in the company
of Peers whose ancestors had been attainted for treason
against the Plantagenets. The envy of the class which 20
Frederic quitted, and the civil scorn of the class into which he
intruded himself, were marked in very significant ways. The
Elector of Saxony at first refused to acknowledge the new
Majesty. Lewis the Fourteenth looked down on his brother
King with an air not unlike that with which the count in 25
Molière's play regards Monsieur Jourdain, just fresh from the

---

3. **Peace of Westphalia.** Concluded in 1648, and made an end of the
Thirty Years' War.

17. **Nabob.** In Macaulay's day a nabob was an Englishman who, having
lived in India all his life, returned to his native land to enjoy a princely
fortune. The commissaries were English officials in India. They were
popularly supposed to have amassed vast riches by grinding down the
natives.

19. **Peers.** Hereditary members of the English House of Lords.

20. **Plantagenets.** The Plantagenets ruled England from 1154 until 1485.
The name was first adopted by Geoffrey, Count of Anjou, husband of Matilda,
the daughter of Henry I., from the sprig of broom (*planta genesta*) which
he wore in his helmet.

26. **Monsieur Jourdain.** Perhaps the best known comedy of Molière,
the great French dramatist, is *Le Bourgeois gentilhomme* (1670). Monsieur
Jourdain, the hero, is an elderly tradesman who, having fallen into a large
fortune, wishes to educate himself to his new position in society. He en-
gages dancing-masters, fencing-masters, and so on. Everyone makes fun

mummery of being made a gentleman. Austria exacted large
sacrifices in return for her recognition, and at last gave it
ungraciously.

Frederic was succeeded by his son, Frederic William, a
5 prince who must be allowed to have possessed some talents for
administration, but whose character was disfigured by odious
vices, and whose eccentricities were such as had never before
been seen out of a madhouse. He was exact and diligent in
the transacting of business ; and he was the first who formed
10 the design of obtaining for Prussia a place among the
European powers, altogether out of proportion to her extent
and population, by means of a strong military organization.
Strict economy enabled him to keep up a peace establishment
of sixty thousand troops. These troops were disciplined in
15 such a manner, that, placed beside them, the household regiments of Versailles and St. James's would have appeared an
awkward squad. The master of such a force could not but be
regarded by all his neighbors as a formidable enemy and a
valuable ally.

20 But the mind of Frederic William was so ill regulated, that
all his inclinations became passions, and all his passions par-
took of the character of moral and intellectual disease. His
parsimony degenerated into sordid avarice. His taste for military pomp and order became a mania, like that of a Dutch
25 burgomaster for tulips, or that of a member of the Roxburghe
Club for Caxtons. While the envoys of the Court of Berlin

---

of him, and finally two of his young acquaintances induce him to go through
a long ceremonial, without which, they tell him, he can never be a true
gentleman. One remark of Monsieur Jourdain is especially famous : he
says he has been talking prose all his life and never knew it until his
professor told him.

16. **The household regiments of Versailles and St. James.** That
is, the royal body-guards at Versailles, and at St. James' Palace in London.

25. **Tulips.** In the years 1636 and 1637 there was a mania in Holland for
tulips, and men speculated in them just as they do now in railroad shares.
Bulbs were sold for enormous sums. For a single tulip bulb the sum of
$7000 was given. The ownership of a bulb was often divided into shares.
These extravagances soon ceased, but not until they had involved many
people in ruin.

26. **Caxtons.** The Roxburghe Club was founded in 1812 in London. Its
object was the reprinting of rare and ancient pieces of literature. The
members were all noted bibliophiles, and spent their time in searching for
old books.

William Caxton (1412-1492). The introducer of printing into England.

were in a state of such squalid poverty as moved the laughter
of foreign capitals, while the food placed before the princes
and princesses of the blood-royal of Prussia was too scanty to
appease hunger, and so bad that even hunger loathed it, no
price was thought too extravagant for tall recruits. The ambi- 5
tion of the King was to form a brigade of giants, and every
country was ransacked by his agents for men above the ordinary stature. These researches were not confined to Europe.
No head that towered above the crowd in the bazaars of
Aleppo, of Cairo, or of Surat, could escape the crimps of Fred- 10
eric William. One Irishman, more than seven feet high, who
was picked up in London by the Prussian ambassador, received
a bounty of near thirteen hundred pounds sterling, very much
more than the ambassador's salary. This extravagance was
the more absurd, because a stout youth of five feet eight, who 15
might have been procured for a few dollars, would in all probability have been a much more valuable soldier. But to Frederic William this huge Irishman was what a brass Otho, or a
Vinegar Bible, is to a collector of a different kind.

It is remarkable, that though the main end of Frederic Will- 20
iam's administration was to have a great military force, though
his reign forms an important epoch in the history of military
discipline, and though his dominant passion was the love of
military display, he was yet one of the most pacific of princes.
We are afraid that his aversion to war was not the effect of 25
humanity, but was merely one of his thousand whims. His
feeling about his troops seems to have resembled a miser's

He learned the art in Belgium, and brought his presses to London in 1474.
The first book printed was *The Game and Playe of Chesse.* A few of his
books are still preserved.

10. **Crimps.** It was a military custom of Frederic's time to send out
recruiting-sergeants or crimps, who would ply their victims with drink and
then induce them to enlist. Carlyle uses the word as a verb: " Coaxing
and courting with intent to crimp him " (*Miscellanies.* iii. 197).

18. **Brass Otho.** A brass coin of the time of Otho the Great, Emperor of
the Holy Roman Empire (912–973).

19. **Vinegar Bible.** A Bible published in 1717 in two volumes. The name
comes from an error in the running-title at St. Luke, ch. xxii., where we read
" the parable of the *vinegar*" instead of " the parable of the vineyard." The
volume is magnificently printed. Soon after its appearance, however, it
was discovered to be carelessly and incorrectly edited. There are only five
copies in existence. It is consequently highly prized by book collectors.

feeling about his money. He loved to collect them, to count them, to see them increase ; but he could not find it in his heart to break in upon the precious hoard. He looked forward to some future time when his Patagonian battalions were
5 to drive hostile infantry before them like sheep : but this future time was always receding ; and it is probable that, if his life had been prolonged thirty years, his superb army would never have seen any harder service than a sham fight in the fields near Berlin. But the great military means which he
10 had collected were destined to be employed by a spirit far more daring and inventive than his own.

Frederic, surnamed the Great, son of Frederic William, was born in January 1712. It may safely be pronounced that he had received from nature a strong and sharp understanding,
15 and a rare firmness of temper and intensity of will. As to the other parts of his character, it is difficult to say whether they are to be ascribed to nature, or to the strange training which he underwent. The history of his boyhood is painfully interesting. Oliver Twist in the parish workhouse, Smike at Dothe-
20 boys Hall, were petted children when compared with this wretched heir-apparent of a crown. The nature of Frederic William was hard and bad, and the habit of exercising arbitrary power had made him frightfully savage. His rage constantly vented itself to right and left in curses and blows.
25 When his Majesty took a walk, every human being fled before him, as if a tiger had broken loose from a menagerie. If he met a lady in the street, he gave her a kick, and told her to go home and mind her brats. If he saw a clergyman staring at the soldiers, he admonished the reverend gentleman to betake
30 himself to study and prayer, and enforced this pious advice by a sound caning, administered on the spot. But it was in his

---

4. **Patagonian.** Mr. Bourne, an American sailor, who was for some time a captive among the savage Patagonians, says that their average height is 6½ feet, while many are over 7 feet tall.

19. **Parish workhouse.** See Dickens's *Oliver Twist*, which was written to expose the cruelties perpetrated on destitute children at the workhouses.

20. **Dotheboys Hall.** See Dickens's *Nicholas Nickleby*. Smike is the domestic drudge at the Squeers Academy. Starved and beaten, he becomes broken-spirited and nearly half witted, when Nicholas Nickleby takes pity on him and helps him to run away.

own house that he was most unreasonable and ferocious. His palace was hell, and he the most execrable of fiends, a cross between Moloch and Puck. His son Frederic and his daughter Wilhelmina, afterwards Margravine of Bareuth, were in an especial manner objects of his aversion. His own mind was 5 uncultivated. He despised literature. He hated infidels, papists, and metaphysicians, and did not very well understand in what they differed from each other. The business of life, according to him, was to drill and to be drilled. The recreations suited to a prince were to sit in a cloud of tobacco 10 smoke, to sip Swedish beer between the puffs of the pipe, to play backgammon for three halfpence a rubber, to kill wild hogs, and to shoot partridges by the thousand. The Prince Royal showed little inclination either for the serious employments or for the amusements of his father. He shirked the 15 duties of the parade : he detested the fume of tobacco : he had no taste either for backgammon or for field sports. He had an exquisite ear, and performed skillfully on the flute. His earliest instructors had been French refugees, and they had awakened in him a strong passion for French literature and 20 French society. Frederic William regarded these tastes as effeminate and contemptible, and, by abuse and persecution, made them still stronger. Things became worse when the Prince Royal attained that time of life at which the great revolution in the human mind and body takes place. He was 25 guilty of some youthful indiscretions, which no good and wise parent would regard with severity. At a later period he was accused, truly or falsely, of vices from which History averts

---

3. **Moloch.** The third in rank of the Satanic hierarchy in Milton's *Paradise Lost.* Satan first, Beelzebub second.

> " First Moloch, horrid king besmeared with blood
> Of human sacrifice, and parents' tears."

The Ammonites sacrificed their children to their brazen idol by laying them in his arms. A hot fire was continually kept burning inside the idol, which would rapidly burn the bodies to ashes.

3. **Puck.** Synonymous with Hobgoblin. Shakespeare in *Midsummer-Night's Dream* represents him as " a very Shetlander among the gossamer-winged, dainty-limbed fairies, strong enough to knock all their heads together, a rough, knurly-limbed, fawn-faced, shock-pated, mischievous little urchin."

her eyes, and which even Satire blushes to name, vices such
that, to borrow the energetic language of Lord Keeper Coventry, "the depraved nature of man, which of itself carrieth
man to all other sin, abhorreth them." But the offenses of
5 his youth were not characterized by any peculiar turpitude.
They excited, however, transports of rage in the King, who
hated all faults except those to which he was himself inclined,
and who conceived that he made ample atonement to Heaven
for his brutality, by holding the softer passions in detestation.
10 The Prince Royal, too, was not one of those who are content to
take their religion on trust. He asked puzzling questions,
and brought forward arguments which seemed to savor of
something different from pure Lutheranism. The King suspected that his son was inclined to be a heretic of some sort or
15 other, whether Calvinist or Atheist his Majesty did not very
well know. The ordinary malignity of Frederic William was
bad enough. He now thought malignity a part of his duty as
a Christian man, and all the conscience that he had stimulated
his hatred. The flute was broken : the French books were
20 sent out of the palace : the Prince was kicked and cudgeled,
and pulled by the hair. At dinner the plates were hurled at
his head : sometimes he was restricted to bread and water :
sometimes he was forced to swallow food so nauseous that he
could not keep it on his stomach. Once his father knocked
25 him down, dragged him along the floor to a window, and was
with difficulty prevented from strangling him with the cord of
the curtain. The Queen, for the crime of not wishing to see
her son murdered, was subjected to the grossest indignities.
The Princess Wilhelmina, who took her brother's part, was
30 treated almost as ill as Mrs. Brownrigg's apprentices. Driven
to despair, the unhappy youth tried to run away. Then the
fury of the old tyrant rose to madness. The Prince was an

---

2. **Lord Thomas Coventry** (1578-1640). An English statesman of great
repute.
30. **Mrs. Brownrigg's apprentices.** In the latter part of the 18th
century a Mrs. Brownrigg murdered one or more of her apprentices. Later,
George Canning, the great statesman, published in the *Anti-Jacobin* a poem
in which Mrs. Brownrigg laments her hard fate. Canning's work was a
parody on one of Robert Southey's early poems.

officer in the army : his flight was therefore desertion ; and, in the moral code of Frederic William, desertion was the highest of all crimes. " Desertion," says this royal theologian, in one of his half-crazy letters, " is from hell. It is a work of the children of the Devil. No child of God could possibly be guilty 5 of it." An accomplice of the Prince, in spite of the recommendation of a court-martial, was mercilessly put to death. It seemed probable that the Prince himself would suffer the same fate. It was with difficulty that the intercession of the States of Holland, of the Kings of Sweden and Poland, and of 10 the Emperor of Germany, saved the House of Brandenburg from the stain of an unnatural murder. After months of cruel suspense, Frederic learned that his life would be spared. He remained, however, long a prisoner ; but he was not on that account to be pitied. He found in his jailers a tender- 15 ness which he had never found in his father ; his table was not sumptuous, but he had wholesome food in sufficient quantity to appease hunger : he could read the Henriade without being kicked, and could play on his flute without having it broken over his head. 20

When his confinement terminated he was a man. He had nearly completed his twenty-first year, and could scarcely be kept much longer under the restraints which had made his boyhood miserable. Suffering had matured his understanding, while it had hardened his heart and soured his temper. He 25 had learned self-command and dissimulation : he affected to conform to some of his father's views, and submissively accepted a wife, who was a wife only in name, from his father's hand. He also served with credit, though without any opportunity of acquiring brilliant distinction, under the command 30 of Prince Eugene, during a campaign marked by no extraor-

---

18. **La Henriade.** An epic poem by Voltaire (1694–1778). It was published fraudulently in an imperfect form as *La Ligue*.

31. **Prince Eugene** (1663–1736). One of the great generals of modern times. Born in Paris, he was intended for the church, and became known as the "little Abbé." He had a passion for military glory, however, and soon left the church to fight against the Turks. So greatly did he distinguish himself that he was given the command of a regiment of dragoons. After this he quickly rose in his chosen profession. The war of the Spanish Succession raised his fame to the highest pitch. He participated largely in the

dinary events. He was now permitted to keep a separate
establishment, and was therefore able to indulge with caution
his own tastes. Partly in order to conciliate the King, and
partly, no doubt, from inclination, he gave up a portion of
5 his time to military and political business, and thus gradually
acquired such an aptitude for affairs as his most intimate
associates were not aware that he possessed.

His favorite abode was at Rheinsberg, near the frontier
which separates the Prussian dominions from the duchy of
10 Mecklenburg. Rheinsberg is a fertile and smiling spot, in the
midst of the sandy waste of the marquisate. The mansion,
surrounded by woods of oak and beech, looks out upon a
spacious lake. There Frederic amused himself by laying out
gardens in regular alleys and intricate mazes, by building
15 obelisks, temples, and conservatories, and by collecting rare
fruits and flowers. His retirement was enlivened by a few
companions, among whom he seems to have preferred those
who, by birth or extraction, were French. With these inmates he dined and supped well, drank freely, and amused
20 himself sometimes with concerts, and sometimes with holding
chapters of a fraternity which he called the Order of Bayard ;
but literature was his chief resource.

His education had been entirely French. The long ascendency which Lewis XIV. had enjoyed, and the eminent merit
25 of the tragic and comic dramatists, of the satirists, and of the
preachers who had flourished under that magnificent prince,
had made the French language predominant in Europe.
Even in countries which had a national literature, and which
could boast of names greater than those of Racine, of

---

victories of Blenheim, Oudenarde, and Malplaquet. Activity, boldness, and
promptitude in repairing his faults were his distinguishing characteristics.
He was no indifferent scholar, and wisely coincided in the opinion of Gustavus Adolphus that a good Christian always makes a good soldier. His
collection of books, pictures, and prints is still preserved.

29. **Jean Racine** (1639-1699). A very eminent French dramatist. His
chief plays are *Alexandre*, *Andromaque*, *Les Plaideurs*, *Britannicus*,
Iphigénie, and *Phèdre*. With the usual fate of French authors, he excited a
strong party against him, which finally induced him to renounce the dramatic art. Many years afterward he was persuaded by Madame de Main-
tenon to write a dramatic piece on a sacred subject. *Esther* was the result,
followed closely by *Athalie*. Besides his dramatic works, Racine was the

Molière, and of Massillon, in the country of Dante, in the country
of Cervantes, in the country of Shakespeare and Milton, the intellectual fashions of Paris had been to a great extent adopted.
Germany had not yet produced a single master-piece of
poetry or eloquence. In Germany, therefore, the French taste 5
reigned without rival and without limit. Every youth of rank
was taught to speak and write French. That he should speak
and write his own tongue with politeness, or even with accuracy
and facility, was regarded as comparatively an unimportant

author of *L'Histoire de Port Royal, Idylle sur la Paix, Epigrams, Letters,*
etc.

1. **Jean Baptiste Poquelin Molière** (1622-1673).   A famous French
comic author and actor. His most celebrated comedies are *Les Précieuses
Ridicules, Le Misanthrope, Tartuffe,* and *Le Bourgeois Gentilhomme.*
Seldom, if ever, has there been a more remarkable instance of the triumph
of genius over the pride of rank. Though only an actor at a time when
the French nobility were proudest and most exclusive, Molière was treated
by them as a friend and companion. Hallam, the eminent critic, says:
"Shakespeare had the greater genius, but perhaps Molière has written the
best comedies." Although Molière was not a member of the French Academy, its learned members after his death placed his bust in their hall, with
this beautiful inscription: "*Rien ne manque à sa gloire, il manquait à la
nôtre*" (Nothing is wanting to his glory, but he was wanting to ours).

1. **Jean Baptiste Massillon** (1663-1742).   A French prelate, and one
of the greatest preachers of all time. He held all Paris enchained by his
eloquence. Eventually his fame became so great that it excited the curiosity of Louis XIV. to hear him. He was appointed to preach a course of
Advent sermons at Versailles. The king was so delighted that he paid him
this fine compliment: "Father, I have often had my pulpit filled by celebrated orators, with whom I have been greatly pleased; but whenever I
hear you, I am much displeased with myself." Massillon's works consist
entirely of sermons and funeral orations.

1. **Dante Alighieri** (1265-1321).   The greatest of Italian poets and the
greatest poetical genius that flourished between the Augustan and the
Elizabethan ages. The *Divina Commedia* is his greatest work.

2. **Miguel de Cervantes Saavedra** (1547-1616).   The greatest name in
Spanish literature is that of the author of the immortal *Don Quixote.*
Cervantes came of an ancient family, which was originally from Gallicia.
He was destined for the ecclesiastical profession, but finding it too slow for
his venturesome taste, he became a soldier of fortune. Cervantes, unlike
most men of great genius, was a very courageous man. He distinguished
himself in several campaigns, but finally was taken captive by that ferocious
corsair Arnaut Marin, who carried him to Algiers, where he was kept in
bondage for four years. At the end of that time he was ransomed and
allowed to return to Spain. In 1605 appeared the first part of *Don Quixote.*
Cervantes at once attained the greatest celebrity. His book was translated
into every language of Europe. The most eminent painters, tapestry-
weavers, engravers, and sculptors were employed in representing the history
of "the sorrowful knight with the metaphysical countenance." Cervantes
received the most distinguished marks of royal favor. As King Philip III.
was standing on a balcony of his palace at Madrid he saw a man walking
outside reading a book, and every now and then bursting into laughter, upon
which the king remarked, "This man is either mad, or reading Don Quixote."
Cervantes wrote a series of novels, that is, short stories, which were the
first written in the Spanish tongue. Besides these, a number of plays,
among which is the tremendous tragedy *Numancia,* are due to Cervantes'
genius.

object.   Even Frederic William, with all his rugged Saxon
prejudices, thought it necessary that his children should know
French, and quite unnecessary that they should be well versed
in German.   The Latin was positively interdicted.   "My son,"
5 his Majesty wrote, "shall not learn Latin ; and, more than
that, I will not suffer anybody even to mention such a thing
to me."   One of the preceptors ventured to read the Golden
Bull in the original with the Prince Royal.   Frederic William
entered the room, and broke out in his usual kingly style.

10   "Rascal, what are you at there ?"

"Please your Majesty," answered the preceptor, "I was ex-
plaining the Golden Bull to his Royal Highness."

"I'll Golden Bull you, you rascal !" roared the Majesty of
Prussia.   Up went the King's cane, away ran the terrified in-
15 structor ; and Frederic's classical studies ended forever.   He
now and then affected to quote Latin sentences, and produced
such exquisitely Ciceronian phrases as these :—"Stante pede
morire,"—"De gustibus non est disputandus,"—"Tot verbas
tot spondera."   Of Italian, he had not enough to read a page
20 of Metastasio with ease ; and of the Spanish and English, he
did not, as far as we are aware, understand a single
word.

As the highest human compositions to which he had access
were those of the French writers, it is not strange that his
25 admiration for those writers should have been unbounded.
His ambitious and eager temper early prompted him to imitate
what he admired.   The wish, perhaps, dearest to his heart
was, that he might rank among the masters of French rhetoric
and poetry.   He wrote prose and verse as indefatigably as if

7. **The Golden Bull.** The fundamental law of the Holy Roman Empire,
by which the election of the emperor was intrusted to seven electors. It
received its name from the gold case which contained the seal. A bull is a
papal edict.

20. **Pietro Bonaventura Metastasio** (1698–1782). A celebrated Italian
poet, whose Greek name means in English, transmutation. He was called
thus from the fact that, when a poor child singing in the streets of Rome,
he attracted the attention of a learned man, who took him to his house and
educated him. He became in time a famous dramatist and poet. Perhaps
his best known work is *La Clemenza di Tito*, which was set to music by
Mozart in 1790.

he had been a starving hack of Cave or Osborn ; but Nature,
which had bestowed on him, in a large measure, the talents of
a captain and of an administrator, had withheld from him
those higher and rarer gifts, without which industry labors
in vain to produce immortal eloquence and song. And, in-5
deed, had he been blessed with more imagination, wit, and
fertility of thought, than he appears to have had, he would
still have been subject to one great disadvantage, which would,
in all probability, have forever prevented him from taking a
high place among men of letters. He had not the full com-10
mand of any language. There was no machine of thought
which he could employ with perfect ease, confidence, and freedom. He had German enough to scold his servants, or to give
the word of command to his grenadiers ; but his grammar and
pronunciation were extremely bad. He found it difficult to 15
make out the meaning even of the simplest German poetry.
On one occasion a version of Racine's Iphigénie was read to
him. He held the French original in his hand ; but was forced
to own that, even with such help, he could not understand the
translation. Yet, though he had neglected his mother tongue 20
in order to bestow all his attention on French, his French was,
after all, the French of a foreigner. It was necessary for him
to have always at his beck some men of letters from Paris to
point out the solecisms and false rhymes of which, to the last,
he was frequently guilty. Even had he possessed the poetic 25
faculty, of which, as far as we can judge, he was utterly destitute, the want of a language would have prevented him from
being a great poet. No noble work of imagination, as far as
we recollect, was ever composed by any man, except in a dia-
lect which he had learned without remembering how or when, 30
and which he had spoken with perfect ease before he had ever
analyzed its structure. Romans of great abilities wrote Greek

---

1. **Edward Cave** (1691-1782). An English printer and publisher, whose
chief claim to fame is that Dr. Johnson wrote his *Life*. He hired poor
starving poets to write for him.
1. **Francis Osborn** (1589-1658). An English miscellaneous writer of
mediocre genius.
17. **Iphigénie.** One of Racine's most famous tragedies.

verses ; but how many of those verses have deserved to live?
Many men of eminent genius have, in modern times, written
Latin poems ; but, as far as we are aware, none of those
poems, not even Milton's, can be ranked in the first class of
5 art, or even very high in the second. It is not strange,
therefore, that, in the French verses of Frederic, we can find
nothing beyond the reach of any man of good parts and industry, nothing above the level of Newdigate and Seatonian
poetry. His best pieces may perhaps rank with the worst in
10 Dodsley's collection. In history, he succeeded better. We do
not indeed find, in any part of his voluminous Memoirs, either
deep reflection or vivid painting. But the narrative is distinguished by clearness, conciseness, good sense, and a certain
air of truth and simplicity, which is singularly graceful in a
15 man who, having done great things, sits down to relate them.
On the whole, however, none of his writings are so agreeable
to us as his Letters, particularly those which are written with
earnestness, and are not embroidered with verses.

It is not strange that a young man devoted to literature,
20 and acquainted only with the literature of France, should
have looked with profound veneration on the genius of
Voltaire. "A man who has never seen the sun," says Calderon, in one of his charming comedies, "cannot be blamed
for thinking that no glory can exceed that of the moon. A
25 man who has seen neither moon nor sun, cannot be blamed

---

8. Oxford and Cambridge Universities offer yearly prizes for poetry.

10. **Robert Dodsley** (1703–1764). An English bookseller, author, and
editor. He was the first collector of old plays and poems.

22. **François Marie Arouet de Voltaire** (1694-1778). A great French
writer and satirist. From his youth Voltaire ranged himself in opposition
to the French government and the accepted religious teachings of the day.
At times he was greatly honored in France, but again he would have to flee
for his life. His chief claim to literary fame rests on his satires, tales,
letters, and epigrams. In these the whole spirit of the age saw itself expressed with inimitable veracity, grace, wit, and agreeableness. Voltaire
was a decided theist. He rebuked the philosophy of his age, which tried to
banish God from the universe. His last words were: "I die, worshiping
God, loving my friends, not hating my enemies, but detesting superstition."

22. **Calderon de la Barca** (1600–1683). A celebrated Spanish dramatic
author. While his works abound in interesting, sublime, and natural
passages, yet there is also much that is absurd or extravagant. He wrote
the tragedies *The Constant Prince* and *The Physician of his own Honor.*
Hallam says: "His total want of truth to nature, even the ideal nature
which poetry embodies, justifies the sentence that he does not belong among
the mighty masters of the dramatic art."

for talking of the unrivaled brightness of the morning star."
Had Frederic been able to read Homer and Milton, or even
Virgil and Tasso, his admiration of the Henriade would prove
that he was utterly destitute of the power of discerning what
is excellent in art. Had he been familiar with Sophocles or 5
Shakespeare, we should have expected him to appreciate Zaire
more justly. Had he been able to study Thucydides and
Tacitus in the original Greek and Latin, he would have known
that there were heights in the eloquence of history far beyond
the reach of the author of the Life of Charles the Twelfth. 10
But the finest heroic poem, several of the most powerful
tragedies, and the most brilliant and picturesque historical
work that Frederic had ever read, were Voltaire's. Such high
and various excellence moved the young Prince almost to
adoration. The opinions of Voltaire on religious and philo- 15
sophical questions had not yet been fully exhibited to the
public. At a later period, when an exile from his country,
and at open war with the Church, he spoke out. But when
Frederic was at Rheinsberg, Voltaire was still a courtier ; and,
though he could not always curb his petulant wit, he had as 20
yet published nothing that could exclude him from Versailles,
and little that a divine of the mild and generous school of
Grotius and Tillotson might not read with pleasure. In the
Henriade, in Zaire, and in Alzire, Christian piety is exhibited

---

3. **Torquato Tasso** (1544–1595). A celebrated Italian epic poet. His
greatest work is *Gerusalemme Liberata*.
5. **Sophocles** (B.C. 495–406). The most celebrated tragic poet that Greece
ever produced. Charles Eliot Norton, the friend of Emerson and Ruskin,
puts Sophocles second only to Shakespeare. Sophocles formulated the
rules of the tragic art. His greatest works are *Antigone, Philoctetes*, and
Œdipus et Colonus.
6. **Zaire.** A tragedy by Voltaire, adapted from Shakespeare's *Othello*.
7. **Thucydides** (B.C. 471–396). The first great historian. He has been
called " the pathfinder of history."
8. **Tacitus** (A.D. 61–118). A great Roman historian. Among other
works he wrote a history of the early Germanic nations, which is invaluable
to modern scholars.
10. **Charles the Twelfth :** by Voltaire.
23. **Hugo Grotius** (1583–1645). A famous Dutch philosopher and poet.
He desired the union of all Christians into one denomination. He was a
shining light of toleration in this period of rigorous, bigoted Christianity.
23. **John Tillotson** (1630–1694). Archbishop of Canterbury, and chief
adviser of King William in all matters pertaining to church government.
24. **Henriade, Zaire, and Alzire.** Works of Voltaire.,

in the most amiable form ; and, some years after the period of which we are writing, a Pope condescended to accept the dedication of Mahomet. The real sentiments of the poet, however, might be clearly perceived by a keen eye through the
5 decent disguise with which he veiled them, and could not escape the sagacity of Frederic, who held similar opinions, and had been accustomed to practice similar dissimulation.

The Prince wrote to his idol in the style of a worshiper ; and Voltaire replied with exquisite grace and address. A
10 correspondence followed, which may be studied with advantage by those who wish to become proficients in the ignoble art of flattery. No man ever paid compliments better than Voltaire. His sweetest confectionery had always a delicate, yet stimulating flavor, which was delightful to palates wearied
15 by the coarse preparations of inferior artists. It was only from his hand that so much sugar could be swallowed without making the swallower sick. Copies of verses, writing-desks, trinkets of amber, were exchanged between the friends. Frederic confided his writings to Voltaire ; and Voltaire
20 applauded, as if Frederic had been Racine and Bossuet in one. One of his Royal Highness's performances was a refutation of Machiavelli. Voltaire undertook to convey it to the press. It was entitled the Anti-Machiavel, and was an edifying homily against rapacity, perfidy, arbitrary government,
25 unjust war—in short, against almost everything for which its author is now remembered among men.

The old King uttered now and then a ferocious growl at the diversions of Rheinsberg. But his health was broken ; his end was approaching ; and his vigor was impaired. He had
30 only one pleasure left, that of seeing tall soldiers. He could

---

3. **Mahomet.** Dedicated to Pope Benedict XIV.
20. **Jacques Bénigne Bossuet** (1627-1704). A celebrated French prelate and preacher. His orations are famous for the beauty and vigor of their literary style.
22. **Nicolo Machiavelli** (1469 1527). An Italian statesman, writer, and diplomatist, whose name became a synonym for perfidy and deceit. He was hated by the Florentines, and banished from the city. Macaulay, however, says : "The name of a man, to whose patriotic wisdom an oppressed people owed their last chance of emancipation, passed into a proverb of infamy."

always be propitiated by a present of a grenadier of six feet four or six feet five ; and such presents were from time to time judiciously offered by his son.

Early in the year 1740, Frederic William met death with a firmness and dignity worthy of a better and wiser man ; and 5 Frederic, who had just completed his twenty-eighth year, became King of Prussia. His character was little understood. That he had good abilities, indeed, no person who had talked with him, or corresponded with him, could doubt. But the easy Epicurean life which he had led, his love of good cookery 10 and good wine, of music, of conversation, of light literature, led many to regard him as a sensual and intellectual voluptuary. His habit of canting about moderation, peace, liberty, and the happiness which a good mind derives from the happiness of others, had imposed on some who should have known 15 better. Those who thought best of him, expected a Telemachus after Fénélon's pattern. Others predicted the approach of a Medicean age, an age propitious to learning and art, and not unpropitious to pleasure. Nobody had the least suspicion that a tyrant of extraordinary military and political 20 talents, of industry more extraordinary still, without fear, without faith, and without mercy, had ascended the throne.

The disappointment of Falstaff at his old boon-companion's

---

10. **Epicurean.** The followers of Epicurus, the great Greek philosopher, believed in taking the greatest possible amount of virtuous pleasure out of life.
16. **Telemachus.** Fénélon draws Telemachus as a model for all men to follow—mild, peaceful, just, brave, and high-minded.
17. **François de Salignac de Fénélon** (1651–1715). A great French prelate. *Les Aventures de Télémaque* (The Adventures of Telemachus) was Fénélon's only work which did not deal entirely with religious matters. This is one of the most popular works in the French language. Fénélon was universally loved and admired throughout Europe for his nobility of character and brilliant mind.
18. **A Medicean age.** The Medici family is renowned for the extraordinary number of powerful statesmen it gave to Italy. Under the rule of the Medicis Florence rose to the highest point of success in the arts and sciences.
23. **Sir John Falstaff.** A famous character in Shakespeare's plays, *King Henry IV.*, parts i. and ii., and *The Merry Wives of Windsor*. In the former he is represented as the boon companion of Henry, Prince of Wales; a soldier, fat, witty, mendacious, and sensual. In the latter he is in love with Mrs. Ford and Mrs. Page, the "Merry Wives." "Falstaff," says Schlegel, the great German philosopher and critic, "is the crown of Shakespeare's comic invention. He is the most agreeable knave that ever was portrayed."

coronation was not more bitter than that which awaited some
of the inmates of Rheinsberg. They had long looked forward
to the accession of their patron, as to the event from which
their own prosperity and greatness was to date. They had at
5 last reached the promised land, the land which they had
figured to themselves as flowing with milk and honey; and
they found it a desert. "No more of these fooleries," was
the short, sharp admonition given by Frederic to one of them.
It soon became plain that, in the most important points, the
10 new sovereign bore a strong family likeness to his predecessor.
There was indeed a wide difference between the father and
the son, as respected extent and rigor of intellect, speculative
opinions, amusements, studies, outward demeanor. But the
groundwork of the character was the same in both. To both
15 were common the love of order, the love of business, the
military taste, the parsimony, the imperious spirit, the temper
irritable even to ferocity, the pleasure in the pain and humiliation of others. But these propensities had in Frederic
William partaken of the general unsoundness of his mind,
20 and wore a very different aspect when found in company with
the strong and cultivated understanding of his successor.
Thus, for example, Frederic was as anxious as any prince
could be about the efficiency of his army. But this anxiety
never degenerated into a monomania, like that which led his
25 father to pay fancy prices for giants. Frederic was as thrifty
about money as any prince or any private man ought to be.
But he did not conceive, like his father, that it was worth
while to eat unwholesome cabbages for the purpose of saving
four or five rixdollars in the year. Frederic was, we fear, as
30 malevolent as his father; but Frederic's wit enabled him
often to show his malevolence in ways more decent than those
to which his father resorted, and to inflict misery and degradation by a taunt instead of a blow. Frederic, it is true, by
no means relinquished his hereditary privilege of kicking and
35 cudgeling. His practice, however, as to that matter, differed
in some important respects from his father's. To Frederic
William, the mere circumstance that any persons whatever,

men, women, or children, Prussians or foreigners, were within reach of his toes and of his cane, appeared to be a sufficient reason for proceeding to belabor them. Frederic required provocation as well as vicinity; nor was he ever known to inflict this paternal species of correction on any but 5 his born subjects; though on one occasion M. Thiébault had reason, during a few seconds, to anticipate the high honor of being an exception to this general rule.

The character of Frederic was still very imperfectly understood either by his subjects or by his neighbors, when events 10 occurred which exhibited it in a strong light. A few months after his accession died Charles VI., Emperor of Germany, the last descendant, in the male line, of the House of Austria.

Charles left no son, and had, long before his death, relinquished all hopes of male issue. During the latter part of 15 his life, his principal object had been to secure to his descendants in the female line the many crowns of the House of Hapsburg. With this view, he had promulgated a new law of succession, widely celebrated throughout Europe under the name of the Pragmatic Sanction. By virtue of this law, his 20 daughter, the Archduchess Maria Theresa, wife of Francis of Loraine, succeeded to the dominions of her ancestors.

No sovereign has ever taken possession of a throne by a clearer title. All the politics of the Austrian cabinet had, during twenty years, been directed to one single end, the settle- 25 ment of the succession. From every person whose rights could be considered as injuriously affected, renunciations in the most solemn form had been obtained. The new law had been ratified by the Estates of all the kingdoms and principalities which made up the great Austrian monarchy. England, 30 France, Spain, Russia, Poland, Prussia, Sweden, Denmark, the Germanic body, had bound themselves by treaty to main-

---

6. **Dieudonné Thiébault.** A French author who had offended Frederic by one of his books.
20. **Pragmatic Sanction.** The term originated in the Byzantine Empire, and signified a public and solemn decree by a prince (*pragmaticos*, "businesslike," later "official"). The name is given to five different treaties.
21. **Maria Theresa.** At this time only twenty-four years of age.

tain the Pragmatic Sanction. That instrument was placed
under the protection of the public faith of the whole civilized
world.

Even if no positive stipulations on this subject had existed,
5 the arrangement was one which no good man would have been
willing to disturb. It was a peaceable arrangement. It was
an arrangement acceptable to the great population whose happiness was chiefly concerned. It was an arrangement which
made no change in the distribution of power among the states
10 of Christendom. It was an arrangement which could be set
aside only by means of a general war; and, if it were set aside,
the effect would be, that the equilibrium of Europe would be
deranged, that the loyal and patriotic feelings of millions
would be cruelly outraged, and that great provinces which had
15 been united for centuries would be torn from each other by
main force.

The sovereigns of Europe were, therefore, bound by every
obligation which those who are intrusted with power over their
fellow-creatures ought to hold most sacred, to respect and de-
20 fend the rights of the Archduchess. Her situation and her
personal qualities were such as might be expected to move the
mind of any generous man to pity, admiration, and chivalrous
tenderness. She was in her twenty-fourth year. Her form
was majestic, her features beautiful, her countenance sweet
25 and animated, her voice musical, her deportment gracious and
dignified. In all domestic relations she was without reproach.
She was married to a husband whom she loved, and was on
the point of giving birth to a child, when death deprived her
of her father. The loss of a parent, and the new cares of
30 empire, were too much for her in the delicate state of her
health. Her spirits were depressed, and her cheek lost its
bloom. Yet it seemed that she had little cause for anxiety.
It seemed that justice, humanity, and the faith of treaties
would have their due weight, and that the settlement so
35 solemnly guaranteed would be quietly carried into effect.
England, Russia, Poland, and Holland, declared in form their
intention to adhere to their engagements. The French min-

isters made a verbal declaration to the same effect. But from no quarter did the young Queen of Hungary receive stronger assurances of friendship and support than from the King of Prussia.

Yet the King of Prussia, the Anti-Machiavel, had already 5 fully determined to commit the great crime of violating his plighted faith, of robbing the ally whom he was bound to defend, and of plunging all Europe into a long, bloody, and desolating war ; and all this for no end whatever, except that he might extend his dominions, and see his name in the 10 gazettes. He determined to assemble a great army with speed and secrecy, to invade Silesia before Maria Theresa should be apprised of his design, and to add that rich province to his kingdom.

We will not condescend to refute at length the pleas which 15 the compiler of the Memoirs before us has copied from Doctor Preuss. They amount to this, that the House of Brandenburg had some ancient pretensions to Silesia, and had in the previous century been compelled, by hard usage on the part of the Court of Vienna, to waive those pretensions. It is certain 20 that, whoever might originally have been in the right, Prussia had submitted. Prince after prince of the House of Brandenburg had acquiesced in the existing arrangement. Nay, the Court of Berlin had recently been allied with that of Vienna, and had guaranteed the integrity of the Austrian states. Is it 25 not perfectly clear that, if antiquated claims are to be set up against recent treaties and long possession, the world can never be at peace for a day? The laws of all nations have wisely established a time of limitation, after which titles, however illegitimate in their origin, cannot be questioned. It is 30 felt by everybody, that to eject a person from his estate on the ground of some injustice committed in the time of the Tudors would produce all the evils which result from arbitrary confiscation, and would make all property insecure. It concerns the

---

5. **Anti-Machiavel.** See note on Machiavelli, p. 24.
17. **Jean David Erdmann Preuss** (1785–1868). A German historian who made deep researches into the period of history which Macaulay is considering.

commonwealth—so runs the legal maxim—that there be an
end of litigation. And surely this maxim is at least equally
applicable to the great commonwealth of states ; for in that
commonwealth litigation means the devastation of provinces,
the suspension of trade and industry, sieges like those of
5 Badajoz and St. Sebastian, pitched fields like those of Eylau
and Borodino. We hold that the transfer of Norway from
Denmark to Sweden was an unjustifiable proceeding ; but
would the King of Denmark be therefore justified in landing,
without any new provocation, in Norway, and commencing
10 military operations there ? The King of Holland thinks, no
doubt, that he was unjustly deprived of the Belgian provinces.
Grant that it were so. Would he, therefore, be justified in
marching with an army on Brussels ? The case against
Frederic was still stronger, inasmuch as the injustice of which
15 he complained had been committed more than a century before. Nor must it be forgotten that he owed the highest personal obligations to the House of Austria. It may be doubted
whether his life had not been preserved by the intercession of
the prince whose daughter he was about to plunder.
20   To do the King justice, he pretended to no more virtue than
he had. In manifestoes he might, for form's sake, insert some
idle stories about his antiquated claim on Silesia ; but in his
conversations and Memoirs he took a very different tone. His
own words are : "Ambition, interest, the desire of making
25 people talk about me, carried the day ; and I decided for war."
  Having resolved on this course, he acted with ability and
vigor. It was impossible wholly to conceal his preparations ;
for throughout the Prussian territories regiments, guns, and
baggage were in motion. The Austrian envoy at Berlin ap-

---

5. **Badajoz and St. Sebastian.** Badajoz in Spain was taken in 1812
by Wellington from the French. St. Sebastian, a town a d fortress in the
north of Spain, was stormed and totally destroyed by Wellington in the
Peninsular War.
  5. **Eylau and Borodino.** The murderous battle of Eylau was in 1807,
between the French under Napoleon, and the Prussians and Russians.
  The battle of Borodino was fought by Napoleon against the Russians near
Moscow. The Russians had permitted Napoleon to approach Moscow without a single battle until the battle of Borodino, where the Russians were
obliged to retire and let the French enter.

prised his court of these facts, and expressed a suspicion of Frederic's designs ; but the ministers of Maria Theresa refused to give credit to so black an imputation on a young prince who was known chiefly by his high professions of integrity and philanthropy. " We will not," they wrote, " we cannot, be- 5 lieve it."

In the mean time the Prussian forces had been assembled. Without any declaration of war, without any demand for reparation, in the very act of pouring forth compliments and assurances of good-will, Frederic commenced hostilities. 10 Many thousands of his troops were actually in Silesia before the Queen of Hungary knew that he had set up any claim to any part of her territories. At length he sent her a message which could be regarded only as an insult. If she would but let him have Silesia, he would, he said, stand by her against 15 any power which should try to deprive her of her other domin- ions ; as if he was not already bound to stand by her, or as if his new promise could be of more value than the old one.

It was the depth of winter. The cold was severe, and the roads heavy with mire. But the Prussians pressed on. Re- 20 sistance was impossible. The Austrian army was then neither numerous nor efficient. The small portion of that army which lay in Silesia was unprepared for hostilities. Glogau was blockaded ; Breslau opened its gates ; Ohlau was evacuated. A few scattered garrisons still held out ; but the whole open 25 country was subjugated : no enemy ventured to encounter the King in the field ; and, before the end of January 1741, he returned to receive the congratulations of his subjects at Berlin.

Had the Silesian question been merely a question between 30 Frederic and Maria Theresa, it would be impossible to acquit the Prussian King of gross perfidy. But when we consider the effects which his policy produced, and could not fail to produce, on the whole community of civilized nations, we are compelled to pronounce a condemnation still more severe. Till he began 35

---

23. **Glogau, Breslau, Ohlau.** Three Silesian fortified towns on the river Oder.

the war, it seemed possible, even probable, that the peace of
the world would be preserved. The plunder of the great
Austrian heritage was indeed a strong temptation ; and in
more than one cabinet ambitious schemes were already medi-
5 tated.   But the treaties by which the Pragmatic Sanction had
been guaranteed were express and recent.   To throw all
Europe into confusion for a purpose clearly unjust, was no
light matter.   England was true to her engagements.   The
voice of Fleury had always been for peace.   He had a con-
10 science.   He was now in extreme old age, and was unwilling,
after a life which, when his situation was considered, must be
pronounced singularly pure, to carry the fresh stain of a great
crime before the tribunal of his God.   Even the vain and
unprincipled Belle-Isle, whose whole life was one wild day-
15 dream of conquest and spoliation, felt that France, bound as
she was by solemn stipulations, could not, without disgrace,
make a direct attack on the Austrian dominions.   Charles,
Elector of Bavaria, pretended that he had a right to a large
part of the inheritance which the Pragmatic Sanction gave to
20 the Queen of Hungary ; but he was not sufficiently powerful to
move without support.   It might, therefore, not unreasonably
be expected that, after a short period of restlessness, all the
potentates of Christendom would acquiesce in the arrangements made by the late Emperor.   But the selfish rapacity of
25 the King of Prussia gave the signal to his neighbors.   His
example quieted their sense of shame.   His success led them
to underrate the difficulty of dismembering the Austrian
monarchy.   The whole world sprang to arms.   On the head
of Frederic is all the blood which was shed in a war which
30 raged during many years and in every quarter of the globe,
the blood of the column of Fontenoy, the blood of the mount-

---

9. **André Hercule de Fleury** (1653–1743). A celebrated French statesman. He was a cardinal, and had the supreme power from 1726–1743. The
king, Louis XV., was completely under his dominance.
14. **Charles Louis Auguste, duc de Belle Isle** (1684–1761). A French
statesman of great ability. It appears that it was through his influence
that France became involved in the general war of 1741.
31. **Fontenoy.** May 5, 1745. Victory of the French over the allies.

aineers who were slaughtered at Culloden. The evils produced by his wickedness were felt in lands where the name of
Prussia was unknown; and, in order that he might rob a
neighbor whom he had promised to defend, black men fought
on the coast of Coromandel, and red men scalped each other 5
by the Great Lakes of North America.

Silesia had been occupied without a battle ; but the Austrian
troops were advancing to the relief of the fortresses which
still held out. In the spring Frederic rejoined his army. He
had seen little of war, and had never commanded any great 10
body of men in the field. It is not, therefore, strange that
his first military operations showed little of that skill which,
at a later period, was the admiration of Europe. What con-
noisseurs say of some pictures painted by Raphael in his youth,
may be said of this campaign. It was in Frederic's early bad 15
manner. Fortunately for him, the generals to whom he was
opposed were men of small capacity. The discipline of his
own troops, particularly of the infantry, was unequaled in
that age ; and some able and experienced officers were at hand
to assist him with their advice. Of these, the most distin- 20
guished was Field-Marshal Schwerin, a brave adventurer of
Pomeranian extraction, who had served half the governments
in Europe, had borne the commissions of the States-General of
Holland and of the Duke of Mecklenburg, had fought under
Marlborough at Blenheim, and had been with Charles the 25
Twelfth at Bender.

Frederic's first battle was fought at Molwitz ; and never did

---

1. **Culloden.** April 16, 1746. Victory of the Duke of Cumberland over
Lord George Murray and the Pretender. This battle was a perfect mas-
sacre.

14. **Raphael Sanzio** (1483–1520). One of the greatest of Italian painters.

25. **John Churchill, Duke of Marlborough** (1650–1722). An English general, whose military genius has been equalled by few men of
modern times. By a marriage with an intimate friend of Queen Anne he
and his wife obtained immense influence over the queen. Marlborough
gained a number of important victories in the War of the Spanish Succession. At Blenheim in Bavaria he utterly crippled the French army, thus
saving Germany from Louis XIV., who was trying to become master of the
whole continent of Europe. Marlborough's other great victories were Ra-
millies in 1706, Oudenarde in 1708, and Malplaquet in 1709.

26. **Charles the Twelfth,** of Sweden. He reigned from 1697 to 1718.
He was obstinate, and in public life under the control of passion. The de-
cline of the power of Sweden is due to his blind obstinacy.

the career of a great commander open in a more inauspicious
manner. His army was victorious. Not only, however, did
he not establish his title to the character of an able general,
but he was so unfortunate as to make it doubtful whether he
5 possessed the vulgar courage of a soldier. The cavalry, which
he commanded in person, was put to flight. Unaccustomed to
the tumult and carnage of a field of battle, he lost his self-
possession, and listened too readily to those who urged him to
save himself. His English gray carried him many miles from
10 the field, while Schwerin, though wounded in two places,
manfully upheld the day. The skill of the old Field-Marshal
and the steadiness of the Prussian battalions prevailed, and
the Austrian army was driven from the field with the loss of
eight thousand men.

15   The news was carried late at night to a mill in which the
King had taken shelter. It gave him a bitter pang. He was
successful ; but he owed his success to dispositions which others
had made, and to the valor of men who had fought while he
was flying. So unpromising was the first appearance of the
20 greatest warrior of that age !

The battle of Molwitz was the signal for a general explosion
throughout Europe. Bavaria took up arms. France, not yet
declaring herself a principal in the war, took part in it as an
ally of Bavaria. The two great statesmen to whom mankind
25 had owed many years of tranquillity, disappeared about this
time from the scene, but not till they had both been guilty of
the weakness of sacrificing their sense of justice and their love
of peace to the vain hope of preserving their power. Fleury,
sinking under age and infirmity, was borne down by the im-
30 petuosity of Belle-Isle. Walpole retired from the service of
his ungrateful country to his woods and paintings at Houghton;
and his power devolved on the daring and eccentric Carteret.

---

30. **Sir Robert Walpole** (1676-1745). A great English statesman. He
occupied many governmental positions, and for twenty years was practically
the only minister. He was much beloved by the people, and entire confidence was reposed in him. His "peace-at any-price" policy secured to
England a long period of great prosperity.
32. **John Carteret, Earl Granville** (1690-1763). An able English
statesman. He was always in opposition to Walpole. " Of all the members

As were the ministers, so were the nations. Thirty years during which Europe had, with few interruptions, enjoyed repose, had prepared the public mind for great military efforts. A new generation had grown up, which could not remember the siege of Turin or the slaughter of Malplaquet; which 5 knew war by nothing but its trophies; and which, while it looked with pride on the tapestries at Blenheim, or the statue in the Place of Victories, little thought by what privations, by what waste of private fortunes, by how many bitter tears, conquests must be purchased. 10

For a time fortune seemed adverse to the Queen of Hungary. Frederic invaded Moravia. The French and Bavarians penetrated into Bohemia and were there joined by the Saxons. Prague was taken. The Elector of Bavaria was raised by the suffrages of his colleagues to the Imperial throne—a throne 15 which the practice of centuries had almost entitled the House of Austria to regard as a hereditary possession.

Yet was the spirit of the haughty daughter of the Cæsars unbroken. Hungary was still hers by an unquestionable title; and, although her ancestors had found Hungary the most 20 mutinous of all their kingdoms, she resolved to trust herself to the fidelity of a people, rude indeed, turbulent, and impatient of oppression, but brave, generous, and simple-hearted. In the midst of distress and peril she had given birth to a son, afterwards the Emperor Joseph the Second. Scarcely had she 25 risen from her couch, when she hastened to Presburg. There, in the sight of an innumerable multitude, she was crowned with the crown and robed with the robe of St. Stephen. No spectator could restrain his tears when the beautiful young

---

of the cabinet," says Macaulay, "Carteret was the most eloquent and accomplished. His talents for debate were of the first order, and his knowledge of foreign affairs superior to that of any living statesman." Carteret always maintained that Hanover should be governed and protected with as much care as England.

5. **Turin.** In 1705, in the War of the Spanish Succession Prince Eugene took Turin, thus obtaining control of Italy.

5. **Malplaquet.** In 1706 Marlborough and Eugene defeated the French at Malplaquet.

28. **Robe of St. Stephen.** Stephen I. was the first important king of Hungary. He was crowned in 1000 A.D., and afterwards was called St. Stephen because of his devotion to the church. His iron crown and robe were preserved and used in all the subsequent coronations.

mother, still weak from child-bearing, rode, after the fashion
of her fathers, up the Mount of Defiance, unsheathed the
ancient sword of state, shook it towards north and south, east
and west, and, with a glow on her pale face, challenged the
5 four corners of the world to dispute her rights and those of
her boy. At the first sitting of the Diet she appeared clad in
deep mourning for her father, and in pathetic and dignified
words implored her people to support her just cause. Magnates
and deputies sprang up, half drew their sabres, and with
10 eager voices vowed to stand by her with their lives and fortunes. Till then, her firmness had never once forsaken her
before the public eye ; but at that shout she sank down upon
her throne, and wept aloud. Still more touching was the
sight when, a few days later, she came again before the Estates
15 of her realm, and held up before them the little Archduke in
her arms. Then it was that the enthusiasm of Hungary broke
forth into that war-cry which soon resounded throughout
Europe, " Let us die for our King, Maria Theresa !"

In the mean time, Frederic was meditating a change of
20 policy. He had no wish to raise France to supreme power on
the Continent, at the expense of the House of Hapsburg. His
first object was to rob the Queen of Hungary. His second
object was that, if possible, nobody should rob her but himself.
He had entered into engagements with the powers leagued
25 against Austria ; but these engagements were in his estimation
of no more force than the guarantee formerly given to the
Pragmatic Sanction. His plan now was to secure his share
of the plunder by betraying his accomplices. Maria Theresa
was little inclined to listen to any such compromise ; but the
30 English government represented to her so strongly the necessity of buying off Frederic, that she agreed to negotiate.
The negotiation would not, however, have ended in a treaty,
had not the arms of Frederic been crowned with a second

2. **Mount of Defiance.** The Mount of Defiance, also called the Royal
Mount, is a small eminence near Presburg.
6. **Diet.** St. Stephen created a national council, consisting of the lords
temporal and spiritual and of the knights or lower nobility. This was the
origin of the later diets.

victory. Prince Charles of Loraine, brother-in-law to Maria Theresa, a bold and active, though unfortunate general, gave battle to the Prussians at Chotusitz, and was defeated. The King was still only a learner of the military art. He acknowledged, at a later period, that his success on this occasion 5 was to be attributed, not at all to his own generalship, but solely to the valor and steadiness of his troops. He completely effaced, however, by his personal courage and energy, the stain which Molwitz had left on his reputation.

A peace, concluded under the English mediation, was the 10 fruit of this battle. Maria Theresa ceded Silesia : Frederic abandoned his allies : Saxony followed his example ; and the Queen was left at liberty to turn her whole force against France and Bavaria. She was everywhere triumphant. The French were compelled to evacuate Bohemia, and with diffi- 15 culty effected their escape. The whole line of their retreat might be tracked by the corpses of thousands who had died of cold, fatigue, and hunger. Many of those who reached their country carried with them the seeds of death. Bavaria was overrun by bands of ferocious warriors from that bloody debat- 20 able land which lies on the frontier between Christendom and Islam. The terrible names of the Pandoor, the Croat, and the Hussar, then first became familiar to western Europe. The unfortunate Charles of Bavaria, vanquished by Austria, betrayed by Prussia, driven from his hereditary states, and 25 neglected by his allies, was hurried by shame and remorse to an untimely end. An English army appeared in the heart of Germany, and defeated the French at Dettingen. The Austrian captains already began to talk of completing the work of Marlborough and Eugene, and of compelling France to relin- 30 quish Alsace and the Three Bishoprics.

The Court of Versailles, in this peril, looked to Frederic for help. He had been guilty of two great treasons ; perhaps he

---

22. **Islam.** The countries whose national religion is Mohammedanism.
22. **Pandoor, Croat, and Hussar.** Fierce soldiers of Southern Hungary.
31. **Alsace and the Three Bishoprics.** By the peace of Westphalia France received the three bishoprics of Metz, Toul, and Verdun, and the greater part of Alsace.

might be induced to commit a third. The Duchess of Cha-
teauroux then held the chief influence over the feeble Lewis.
She determined to send an agent to Berlin ; and Voltaire was
selected for the mission. He eagerly undertook the task ; for,
5 while his literary fame filled all Europe, he was troubled with
a childish craving for political distinction. He was vain, and
not without reason, of his address, and of his insinuating
eloquence ; and he flattered himself that he possessed boundless influence over the King of Prussia. The truth was that
10 he knew, as yet, only one corner of Frederic's character. He
was well acquainted with all the petty vanities and affectations
of the poetaster ; but was not aware that these foibles were
united with all the talents and vices which lead to success in
active life, and that the unlucky versifier who pestered him
15 with reams of middling Alexandrines was the most vigilant,
suspicious, and severe of politicians.

Voltaire was received with every mark of respect and friendship, was lodged in the palace, and had a seat daily at the
royal table. The negotiation was of an extraordinary descrip-
20 tion. Nothing can be conceived more whimsical than the con-
ferences which took place between the first literary man and
the first practical man of the age, whom a strange weakness
had induced to exchange their parts. The great poet would
talk of nothing but treaties and guarantees, and the great
25 King of nothing but metaphors and rhymes. On one occasion
Voltaire put into his Majesty's hands a paper on the state of
Europe, and received it back with verses scrawled on the mar-
gin. In secret they both laughed at each other. Voltaire
did not spare the King's poems ; and the King has left on
30 record his opinion of Voltaire's diplomacy : "He had no cre-
dentials," says Frederic, "and the whole mission was a joke, a
mere farce."

But what the influence of Voltaire could not effect, the
rapid progress of the Austrian arms effected. If it should be
35 in the power of Maria Theresa and George the Second to dictate terms of peace to France, what chance was there that
Prussia would long retain Silesia ? Frederic's conscience told

him that he had acted perfidiously and inhumanly towards the Queen of Hungary. That her resentment was strong she had given ample proof ; and of her respect for treaties he judged by his own. Guarantees, he said, were mere filigree, pretty to look at, but too brittle to bear the slightest pressure. He 5 thought it his safest course to ally himself closely to France, and again to attack the Empress Queen. Accordingly, in the autumn of 1744, without notice, without any decent pretext, he recommenced hostilities, marched through the electorate of Saxony without troubling himself about the permission of the 10 Elector, invaded Bohemia, took Prague, and even menaced Vienna.

It was now that, for the first time, he experienced the inconstancy of fortune. An Austrian army under Charles of Loraine threatened his communications with Silesia. Saxony was all 15 in arms behind him. He found it necessary to save himself by a retreat. He afterwards owned that his failure was the natural effect of his own blunders. No general, he said, had ever committed greater faults. It must be added, that to the reverses of this campaign he always ascribed his subsequent suc- 20 cesses. It was in the midst of difficulty and disgrace that he caught the first clear glimpse of the principles of the military art.

The memorable year 1745 followed. The war raged by sea and land, in Italy, in Germany, and in Flanders ; and even 25 England, after many years of profound internal quiet, saw, for the last time, hostile armies set in battle array against each other. This year is memorable in the life of Frederic, as the date at which his novitiate in the art of war may be said to have terminated. There have been great captains whose pre- 30 cocious and self-taught military skill resembled intuition. Condé, Clive, and Napoleon are examples. But Frederic was

---

32. **Louis, Prince de Condé** (1621–1686). A great French general. During the first part of his military career he fought for Spain, but finally entered the French service. He was not as successful as when fighting for Spain. " He was born a general," says Voltaire; " the art of war seemed in him a natural instinct."

32. **Robert Clive, Baron of Plassey** (1725–1774). A distinguished figure in Anglo-Indian politics. He seemed to have a natural genius for

not one of these brilliant portents. His proficiency in military
science was simply the proficiency which a man of vigorous
faculties makes in any science to which he applies his mind
with earnestness and industry. It was at Hohenfriedberg
5 that he first proved how much he had profited by his errors,
and by their consequences. His victory on that day was
chiefly due to his skillful dispositions, and convinced Europe
that the prince who, a few years before, had stood aghast in
the rout of Molwitz, had attained in the military art a mastery
10 equalled by none of his contemporaries, or equalled by Saxe
alone. The victory of Hohenfriedberg was speedily followed
by that of Sorr.

In the mean time, the arms of France had been victorious in
the Low Countries. Frederic had no longer reason to fear
15 that Maria Theresa would be able to give law to Europe, and
he began to meditate a fourth breach of his engagements.
The Court of Versailles was alarmed and mortified. A letter
of earnest expostulation, in the handwriting of Lewis, was sent
to Berlin ; but in vain. In the autumn of 1745, Frederic
20 made peace with England, and, before the close of the year,
with Austria also. The pretensions of Charles of Bavaria
could present no obstacle to an accommodation. That unhappy prince was no more ; and Francis of Loraine, the husband of Maria Theresa, was raised, with the general assent of
25 the Germanic body, to the Imperial throne.

Prussia was again at peace ; but the European war lasted

---

arms. At thirty years of age Colonel Clive won the famous victory of
Plassey in India, with 3200 men against an army of 50,000 foot, 18,000 horse, 50
pieces of cannon, and a number of elephants. This victory decided the East
India Company's success in India, but it left a stain on the honor of Clive.
He had engaged an eminent merchant to help him in his dispositions for the
campaign, with the promise of a large reward in the event of success. After
the battle Clive said that this agreement had been fictitious, and refused to
pay. By this victory he received from Meer Jaffier, an Indian prince, a gift
of over $1,000,000, and besides this later on he received an annuity of over
$125,000. When he returned to England for the last time a party in the
House of Commons attacked him by moving " that, in the acquisition of his
wealth, Lord Clive had abused the powers with which he was intrusted."
The House rejected this motion, and resolved that " he had rendered great
and meritorious services to his country." But this slur on his honor was
more than Clive could bear, and in 1774 he committed suicide. Lord Chatham happily characterized him as " a heaven-born general, who, without
experience, surpassed all the officers of his time."

18. **Lewis,** i.e., Louis XIV.

till, in the year 1748, it was terminated by the treaty of Aix-la-Chapelle. Of all the powers that had taken part in it, the only gainer was Frederic. Not only had he added to his patrimony the fine province of Silesia : he had, by his unprincipled dexterity, succeeded so well in alternately depressing the 5 scale of Austria and that of France, that he was generally regarded as holding the balance of Europe, a high dignity for one who ranked lowest among kings, and whose great-grandfather had been no more than a Margrave. By the public, the King of Prussia was considered as a politician destitute 10 alike of morality and decency, insatiably rapacious, and shamelessly false ; nor was the public much in the wrong. He was at the same time allowed to be a man of parts, a rising general, a shrewd negotiator and administrator. Those qualities wherein he surpassed all mankind, were as yet unknown 15 to others or to himself ; for they were qualities which shine out only on a dark ground. His career had hitherto, with little interruption, been prosperous ; and it was only in adversity, in adversity which seemed without hope or resource, in adversity which would have overwhelmed even men celebrated 20 for strength of mind, that his real greatness could be shown.

He had, from the commencement of his reign, applied himself to public business after a fashion unknown among kings. Lewis XIV., indeed, had been his own prime minister, and had exercised a general superintendence over all the depart- 25 ments of the government ; but this was not sufficient for Frederic. He was not content with being his own prime minister : he would be his own sole minister. Under him there was no room, not merely for a Richelieu or a Mazarin, but for

9. **Margrave.** One of the lower orders of German nobility.
24. **His own Prime Minister.** It was Louis XIV. who said, " L'état c'est moi " (" I am the state)."
29. **Armand Jean du Plessis, Cardinal, duc de Richelieu** (1585-1642). One of the greatest statesmen France has ever seen. He was first minister in the reign of Louis XIII., in spite of the personal antipathy which the king showed toward him. He alone practically governed France at this time. His political tenets were the unification of France and the destruction of the Austrian royal house. During all Richelieu's long ascendancy continual plots and conspiracies were directed against him, and it was only by force of his extraordinary power of intellect that he was able to keep the reins of government in his own hands.
29. **Jules Mazarin** (1602-1661). Like Richelieu, Mazarin was a prince of

a Colbert, a Louvois, or a Torcy. A love of labor for its own
sake, a restless and insatiable longing to dictate, to inter-
meddle, to make his power felt, a profound scorn and distrust
of his fellow-creatures, made him unwilling to ask counsel, to
5 confide important secrets, to delegate ample powers. The
highest functionaries under his government were mere clerks,
and were not so much trusted by him as valuable clerks are
often trusted by the heads of departments. He was his own
treasurer, his own commander-in-chief, his own intendant of
10 public works, his own minister for trade and justice, for home
affairs and foreign affairs, his own master of the horse,
steward, and chamberlain. Matters of which no chief of an
office in any other government would ever hear, were, in this
singular monarchy, decided by the King in person. If a
15 traveler wished for a good place to see a review, he had to
write to Frederic, and received next day, from a royal messen-
ger, Frederic's answer signed by Frederic's own hand. This
was an extravagant, a morbid activity. The public business
would assuredly have been better done if each department had
20 been put under a man of talents and integrity, and if the King
had contented himself with a general control. In this manner
the advantages which belong to unity of design, and the ad-

---

the church and a great statesman. By his services, first in the Papal army
and afterwards as a diplomat, he had attracted the attention of Richelieu,
who at his death recommended Mazarin as his successor. After the death
of Louis XIII. Mazarin retained his power owing to the influence he had obtained over the French queen, Anne of Austria. Voltaire says " he had that
power over the queen which a sagacious man ought to possess over a
woman who is weak enough to be dominated and strong enough to persist
in her choice of a favorite." Mazarin obtained for himself by his bad
government the hatred of the nobility, the parliament, and the people. He
always triumphed over his enemies in the end, however, and died the master
of France. Some historians hold that he was secretly married to Anne of
Austria, and that the famous " Man in the Iron Mask " was their son.

1. **Jean-Baptiste Colbert, Marquis de Seignelay** (1619–1683). A
great French statesman who under Lewis XIV. was charged with the whole
internal administration of France. He subjected agriculture to the most
minute restrictions, and raised France industrially to a high pitch of prosperity. He was a most accomplished financier.

1. **François-Michel le Tellier, Marquis de Louvois** (1639–1691).
Louvois exercised the same regulating influence over the army that Colbert
exercised over the finances of France.

1. **Jean-Baptiste de Torcy** (1665–1746). A French statesman of great
influence during the regency before Lewis XV. attained his majority. "He
was a good and strong man, with all the qualities necessary to make himself
respected and feared."—*Saint Simon,*

vantages which belong to the division of labor, would have been to a great extent combined. But such a system would not have suited the peculiar temper of Frederic. He could tolerate no will, no reason, in the state, save his own. He wished for no abler assistance than that of penmen who had just understanding enough to translate and transcribe, to make out his scrawls, and to put his concise Yes and No into an official form. Of the higher intellectual faculties, there is as much in a copying machine, or a lithographic press, as he required from a secretary of the cabinet.

His own exertions were such as were hardly to be expected from a human body or a human mind. At Potsdam, his ordinary residence, he rose at three in summer and four in winter. A page soon appeared, with a large basket full of all the letters which had arrived for the King by the last courier, dispatches from ambassadors, reports from officers of revenue, plans of buildings, proposals for draining marshes, complaints from persons who thought themselves aggrieved, applications from persons who wanted titles, military commissions, and civil situations. He examined the seals with a keen eye; for he was never for a moment free from the suspicion that some fraud might be practiced on him. Then he read the letters, divided them into several packets, and signified his pleasure, generally by a mark, often by two or three words, now and then by some cutting epigram. By eight he had generally finished this part of his task. The adjutant-general was then in attendance, and received instructions for the day as to all the military arrangements of the kingdom. Then the King went to review his guards, not as kings ordinarily review their guards, but with the minute attention and severity of an old drill-sergeant. In the mean time the four cabinet secretaries had been employed in answering the letters on which the King had that morning signified his will. These unhappy men were forced to work all the year round like negro slaves in the time of the sugar-crop. They never had a holiday. They never knew what it was to dine. It was necessary that, before they stirred, they should finish the whole of their work. The King, always on his guard

against treachery, took from the heap a handful of letters at
random, and looked into them to see whether his instructions
had been exactly followed. This was no bad security against
foul play on the part of the secretaries ; for if one of them
5 were detected in a trick, he might think himself fortunate if
he escaped with five years of imprisonment in a dungeon.
Frederic then signed the replies, and all were sent off the same
evening.

The general principles on which this strange government
10 was conducted, deserve attention. The policy of Frederic
was essentially the same as his father's ; but Frederic, while
he carried that policy to lengths to which his father never
thought of carrying it, cleared it at the same time from the
absurdities with which his father had encumbered it. The
15 King's first object was to have a great, efficient, and well-
trained army. He had a kingdom which in extent and population was hardly in the second rank of European powers ;
and yet he aspired to a place not inferior to that of the
sovereigns of England, France, and Austria. For that end it
20 was necessary that Prussia should be all sting. Lewis XV.,
with five times as many subjects as Frederic, and more than
five times as large a revenue, had not a more formidable
army. The proportion which the soldiers in Prussia bore to
the people seems hardly credible. Of the males in the vigor
25 of life, a seventh part were probably under arms ; and this
great force had, by drilling, by reviewing, and by the unspar-
ing use of cane and scourge, been taught to perform all
evolutions with a rapidity and a precision which would have
astonished Villars or Eugene. The elevated feelings which
30 are necessary to the best kind of army were then wanting to
the Prussian service. In those ranks were not found the religious and political enthusiasm which inspired the pikemen of
Cromwell, the patriotic ardor, the thirst of glory, the devo-

---

29. **Claude Louis, Duc de Villars** (1653-1734). A celebrated French
general. At the great battle of Malplaquet, in 1709, he was defeated by the
combined forces of Marlborough and Prince Eugene. This was practically
his only defeat.
29. **Eugene.** See note, page 17.
32. **Pikemen of Cromwell.** The English foot-soldiers of Cromwell's

tion to a great leader, which inflamed the Old Guard of
Napoleon. But in all the mechanical parts of the military
calling, the Prussians were as superior to the English and
French troops of that day, as the English and French troops
to a rustic militia.   5

Though the pay of the Prussian soldier was small, though
every rixdollar of extraordinary charge was scrutinized by
Frederic with a vigilance and suspicion such as Mr. Joseph
Hume never brought to the examination of an army estimate,
the expense of such an establishment was, for the means of   10
the country, enormous. In order that it might not be utterly
ruinous, it was necessary that every other expense should be
cut down to the lowest possible point. Accordingly Frederic,
though his dominions bordered on the sea, had no navy. He
neither had nor wished to have colonies. His judges, his   15
fiscal officers, were meanly paid. His ministers at foreign
courts walked on foot, or drove shabby old carriages till the
axle-trees gave way. Even to his highest diplomatic agents,
who resided at London and Paris, he allowed less than a
thousand pounds sterling a year. The royal household was   20
managed with a frugality unusual in the establishments of
opulent subjects, unexampled in any other palace. The King
loved good eating and drinking, and during great part of his
life took pleasure in seeing his table surrounded by guests ;
yet the whole charge of his kitchen was brought within the   25
sum of two thousand pounds sterling a-year. He examined
every extraordinary item with a care which might be thought
to suit the mistress of a boarding-house better than a great
prince. When more than four rixdollars were asked of him
for a hundred oysters, he stormed as if he had heard that one 30

---

time were armed with long pikes or spears, which were largely used to re-
pulse cavalry attacks; the soldiers kneeling, and opposing a bristling array
of spears to the charging horsemen.
    1. **Old Guard of Napoleon.** The Old Guard was composed of veteran
soldiers who were considered the flower of the French army.
    7. **Rixdollar.** This word is derived from the German *Reichsthaler*, a
dollar of the empire. It is valued at about 37 cents.
    9. **Joseph Hume** (1777–1855). A British statesman pre-eminent for many
years in the House of Commons as a financial reformer and as a sturdy
opponent of monopolies and high taxes.

of his generals had sold a fortress to the Empress Queen. Not a bottle of champagne was uncorked without his express order. The game of the royal parks and forests, a serious head of expenditure in most kingdoms, was to him a source 5 of prófit. The whole was farmed out; and, though the farmers were almost ruined by their contract, the King would grant them no remission. His wardrobe consisted of one fine gala dress, which lasted him all his life; of two or three old coats fit for Monmouth Street, of yellow waistcoats soiled with 10 snuff, and of huge boots embrowned by time. One taste alone sometimes allured him beyond the limits of parsimony, nay, even beyond the limits of prudence, the taste for build- ing. In all other things his economy was such as we might call by a harsher name, if we did not reflect that his funds 15 were drawn from a heavily taxed people, and that it was im- possible for him, without excessive tyranny, to keep up at once a formidable army and a splendid court.

Considered as an administrator, Frederic had undoubtedly many titles to praise. Order was strictly maintained through- 20 out his dominions. Property was secure. A great liberty of speaking and of writing was allowed. Confident in the irresistible strength derived from a great army, the King looked down on malcontents and libelers with a wise dis- dain; and gave little encouragement to spies and informers. 25 When he was told of the disaffection of one of his subjects, he merely asked, "How many thousand men can he bring into the field?" He once saw a crowd staring at something on a wall. He rode up, and found that the object of curiosity was a scurrilous placard against himself. The placard had been 30 posted up so high that it was not easy to read it. Frederic ordered his attendants to take it down and put it lower. "My people and I," he said, "have come to an agreement which satisfies us both. They are to say what they please, and I am to do what I please." No person would have dared

---

9. **Monmouth Street.** A street in London, called by Dickens, from its shops for old clothes, " the burial-place of the fashions." " With awestruck heart I walk through that Monmouth Street, with its empty suits, as through a Sanhedrim of stainless ghosts."—*Carlyle.*

to publish in London satires on George II. approaching to the
atrocity of those satires on Frederic, which the booksellers at
Berlin sold with impunity. One bookseller sent to the palace
a copy of the most stinging lampoon that perhaps was ever
written in the world, the Memoirs of Voltaire, published by 5
Beaumarchais, and asked for his Majesty's orders. "Do not
advertise it in an offensive manner," said the King; "but sell
it by all means. I hope it will pay you well." Even among
statesmen accustomed to the license of a free press, such
steadfastness of mind as this is not very common. 10

It is due also to the memory of Frederic to say, that he
earnestly labored to secure to his people the great blessing of
cheap and speedy justice. He was one of the first rulers who
abolished the cruel and absurd practice of torture. No sentence of death, pronounced by the ordinary tribunals, was 15
executed without his sanction; and his sanction, except in
cases of murder, was rarely given. Towards his troops he
acted in a very different manner. Military offenses were
punished with such barbarous scourging, that to be shot was
considered by the Prussian soldier as a secondary punishment. 20
Indeed, the principle which pervaded Frederic's whole policy
was this, that the more severely the army is governed, the
safer it is to treat the rest of the community with lenity.

Religious persecution was unknown under his government,
unless some foolish and unjust restrictions which lay upon the 25
Jews may be regarded as forming an exception. His policy
with respect to the Catholics of Silesia presented an honorable
contrast to the policy which, under very similar circumstances,
England long followed with respect to the Catholics of Ireland.
Every form of religion and irreligion found an asylum in his 30
states. The scoffer whom the parliaments of France had
sentenced to a cruel death, was consoled by a commission in
the Prussian service. The Jesuit who could show his face

---

33. The Jesuits. A religious order founded in 1534 by Ignatius Loyola.
The members of the order took vows of implicit obedience to their superior.
They were largely missionaries. Among the Indians in Canada they gained
great influence. In Europe they served political purposes to such an extent
that they became universally feared and contemned.

nowhere else, who in Britain was still subject to penal laws, who was proscribed by France, Spain, Portugal, and Naples, who had been given up even by the Vatican, found safety and the means of subsistence in the Prussian dominions.

5   Most of the vices of Frederic's administration resolve themselves into one vice, the spirit of meddling. The indefatigable activity of his intellect, his dictatorial temper, his military habits, all inclined him to this great fault. He drilled his people as he drilled his grenadiers. Capital and industry
10   were diverted from their natural direction by a crowd of preposterous regulations. There was a monopoly of coffee, a monopoly of tobacco, a monopoly of refined sugar. The public money, of which the King was generally so sparing, was lavishly spent in plowing bogs, in planting mulberry-trees
15   amidst the sand, in bringing sheep from Spain to improve the Saxon wool, in bestowing prizes for fine yarn, in building manufactories of porcelain, manufactories of carpets, manufactories of hardware, manufactories of lace. Neither the experience of other rulers, nor his own, could ever teach him
20   that something more than an edict and a grant of public money was required to create a Lyons, a Brussels, or a Birmingham.

For his commercial policy, however, there was some excuse. He had on his side illustrious examples and popular prejudice.
25   Grievously as he erred, he erred in company with his age. In other departments his meddling was altogether without apology. He interfered with the course of justice as well as with the course of trade ; and set up his own crude notions of equity against the law as expounded by the unanimous voice
30   of the gravest magistrates. It never occurred to him that men whose lives were passed in adjudicating on questions of civil right, were more likely to form correct opinions on such questions than a prince whose attention was divided among a

---

3. **The Vatican.** A noble assemblage of buildings at the foot of one of the seven hills upon which Rome is built. It includes the Pope's palace, a museum, and a library. The word is also used, as here, to mean the papal party.
21. **Lyons, Brussels, Birmingham.** Flourishing commercial cities.

thousand objects, and who had never read a law-book through. The resistance opposed to him by the tribunals inflamed him to fury. He reviled his Chancellor. He kicked the shins of his Judges. He did not, it is true, intend to act unjustly. He firmly believed that he was doing right, and defending the 5 cause of the poor against the wealthy. Yet this well-meant meddling probably did far more harm than all the explosions of his evil passions during the whole of his long reign. We could make shift to live under a debauchee or a tyrant; but to be ruled by a busybody is more than human nature can bear. 10

The same passion for directing and regulating appeared in every part of the King's policy. Every lad of a certain station in life was forced to go to certain schools within the Prussian dominions. If a young Prussian repaired, though but for a few weeks, to Leyden or Göttingen for the purpose of study, 15 the offense was punished with civil disabilities, and sometimes with the confiscation of property. Nobody was to travel without the royal permission. If the permission were granted, the pocket-money of the tourist was fixed by royal ordinance. A merchant might take with him two hundred and fifty rix- 20 dollars in gold, a noble was allowed to take four hundred; for it may be observed, in passing, that Frederic studiously kept up the old distinction between the nobles and the community. In speculation he was a French philosopher, but in action a German prince. He talked and wrote about the 25 privileges of blood in the style of Siêyes; but in practice no chapter in the empire looked with a keener eye to genealogies and quarterings.

Such was Frederic the Ruler. But there was another Frederic, the Frederic of Rheinsberg, the fiddler and flute-player, 30 the poetaster and metaphysician. Amidst the cares of state the King had retained his passion for music, for reading, for

---

26. **Emmanuel Joseph Sieyès** (1748–1836). A famous French politician and revolutionist. He took prominent parts in all the revolutionary movements in France from 1789 until 1799. He always steered a moderate course, and was one of the few men who were prominent during the French Revolution without losing their heads and fortunes. He was called " the constitution-maker."

writing, for literary society. To these amusements he devoted all the time that he could snatch from the business of war and government; and perhaps more light is thrown on his character by what passed during his hours of relaxation, than
5 by his battles or his laws.

It was the just boast of Schiller that, in his country, no Augustus, no Lorenzo, had watched over the infancy of poetry. The rich and energetic language of Luther, driven by the Latin from the schools of pedants, and by the French
10 from the palaces of kings, had taken refuge among the people. Of the powers of that language Frederic had no notion. He generally spoke of it, and of those who used it, with the contempt of ignorance. His library consisted of French books; at his table nothing was heard but French conversation. The
15 associates of his hours of relaxation were, for the most part, foreigners. Britain furnished to the royal circle two distinguished men, born in the highest rank, and driven by civil dissensions from the land to which, under happier circumstances, their talents and virtues might have been a source
20 of strength and glory. George Keith, Earl Marischal of Scotland, had taken arms for the House of Stuart in 1715; and his younger brother James, then only seventeen years old, had fought gallantly by his side. When all was lost they retired together to the Continent, roved from country to coun-
25 try, served under various standards, and so bore themselves as to win the respect and good-will of many who had no love

---

6. **Johann Christoph Friedrich von Schiller** (1759–1805). One of Germany's great national poets. His greatest dramatic works are: *The Robbers*, *Wallenstein*, *The Maid of Orleans*, *Mary Stuart*, and *William Tell*.

7. **Augustus Cæsar** (63 B.C.–14 A.D.). During the reign of Augustus, Rome reached the highest point of civilization. He protected and encouraged literature and the arts.

7. **Lorenzo de' Medici** (1448–1492). Surnamed the Magnificent. Florence enjoyed great prosperity under Lorenzo. He was highly distinguished as a patron of the arts and literature, and founded at Florence an academy for the study of the antique. He collected a magnificent library and expended large sums in beautifying his city.

8. **Martin Luther** (1483–1546). The great leader of the Reformation in Germany. In 1534 Luther translated the New and Old Testaments into German. These translations, by the force and beauty of their language, exerted a great influence on the growth of the German tongue. From Luther's time dates the modern German language. It was he who shaped it into its present form.

for the Jacobite cause. Their long wanderings terminated at
Potsdam; nor had Frederic any associates who deserved or
obtained so large a share of his esteem. They were not only
accomplished men, but nobles and warriors, capable of serv-
ing him in war and diplomacy, as well as amusing him at 5
supper. Alone of all his companions they appear never to
have had reason to complain of his demeanor towards them.
Some of those who knew the palace best, pronounced that
Lord Marischal was the only human being whom Frederic
ever really loved. 10

Italy sent to the parties at Potsdam the ingenious and
amiable Algarotti, and Bastiani, the most crafty, cautious,
and servile of Abbés. But the greater part of the society
which Frederic had assembled round him was drawn from
France. Maupertuis had acquired some celebrity by the 15
journey which he had made to Lapland, for the purpose of
ascertaining, by actual measurement, the shape of our planet.
He was placed in the Chair of the Academy of Berlin, a
humble imitation of the renowned Academy of Paris. Baculard D'Arnaud, a young poet, who was thought to have 20
given promise of great things, had been induced to quit his
country, and to reside at the Prussian Court. The Marquess
D'Argens was among the King's favorite companions, on
account, as it should seem, of the strong opposition between
their characters. The parts of D'Argens were good, and his 25
manners those of a finished French gentleman; but his
whole soul was dissolved in sloth, timidity, and self-indul-
gence. His was one of that abject class of minds which are
superstitious without being religious. Hating Christianity
with a rancor which made him incapable of rational inquiry, 30
unable to see in the harmony and beauty of the universe the
traces of divine power and wisdom, he was the slave of
dreams and omens, would not sit down to table with thirteen
in company, turned pale if the salt fell towards him, begged
his guests not to cross their knives and forks on their plates, 35

1. **Jacobite cause.** The cause of James II. (Lat. *Jacobus*) and his descendants. The cause of the House of Stuart.

and would not for the world commence a journey on Friday.
His health was a subject of constant anxiety to him. Whenever his head ached, or his pulse beat quick, his dastardly fears
and effeminate precautions were the jest of all Berlin. All
5 this suited the King's purpose admirably. He wanted some-
body by whom he might be amused, and whom he might de-
spise. When he wished to pass half an hour in easy polished
conversation, D'Argens was an excellent companion ; when he
wanted to vent his spleen and contempt, D'Argens was an
10 excellent butt.

With these associates, and others of the same class, Frederic loved to spend the time which he could steal from public
cares. He wished his supper-parties to be gay and easy. He
invited his guests to lay aside all restraint, and to forget that
15 he was at the head of a hundred and sixty thousand soldiers,
and was absolute master of the life and liberty of all who sat
at meat with him. There was, therefore, at these parties the
outward show of ease. The wit and learning of the company
were ostentatiously displayed. The discussions on history and
20 literature were often highly interesting. But the absurdity of
all the religions known among men was the chief topic of conversation ; and the audacity with which doctrines and names
venerated throughout Christendom were treated on these occasions, startled even persons accustomed to the society of French
25 and English freethinkers. Real liberty, however, or real
affection, was in this brilliant society not to be found. Absolute kings seldom have friends : and Frederic's faults were
such as, even where perfect equality exists, make friendship
exceedingly precarious. He had indeed many qualities which,
30 on a first acquaintance, were captivating. His conversation
was lively ; his manners, to those whom he desired to please,
were even caressing. No man could flatter with more delicacy.
No man succeeded more completely in inspiring those who
approached him with vague hopes of some great advantage
35 from his kindness. But under this fair exterior he was a
tyrant, suspicious, disdainful, and malevolent. He had one
taste which may be pardoned in a boy, but which, when

habitually and deliberately indulged by a man of mature age
and strong understanding, is almost invariably the sign of a
bad heart—a taste for severe practical jokes. If a courtier
was fond of dress, oil was flung over his richest suit. If he
was fond of money, some prank was invented to make him 5
disburse more than he could spare. If he was hypochondriacal,
he was made to believe that he had the dropsy. If he had
particularly set his heart on visiting a place, a letter was
forged to frighten him from going thither. These things, it
may be said, are trifles. They are so ; but they are indications, 10
not to be mistaken, of a nature to which the sight of human
suffering and human degradation is an agreeable excitement.

Frederic had a keen eye for the foibles of others, and loved
to communicate his discoveries. He had some talent for sarcasm, and considerable skill in detecting the sore places where 15
sarcasm would be most acutely felt. His vanity, as well as
his malignity, found gratification in the vexation and confusion of those who smarted under his caustic jests. Yet in
truth his success on these occasions belonged quite as much to
the King as to the wit. We read that Commodus descended, 20
sword in hand, into the arena against a wretched gladiator,
armed only with a foil of lead, and, after shedding the blood
of the helpless victim, struck medals to commemorate the
inglorious victory. The triumphs of Frederic in the war of
repartee were of much the same kind. How to deal with him 25
was the most puzzling of questions. To appear constrained in
his presence was to disobey his commands, and to spoil his
amusement. Yet if his associates were enticed by his gracious-
ness to indulge in the familiarity of a cordial intimacy, he was
certain to make them repent of their presumption by some 30
cruel humiliation. To resent his affronts was perilous ; yet
not to resent them was to deserve and to invite them. In his
view, those who mutinied were insolent and ungrateful ; those
who submitted were curs made to receive bones and kickings
with the same fawning patience. It is, indeed, difficult to 35

---

20. **Commodus** (161-192 A.D.). A Roman emperor notorious for his bestial
vices.

conceive how anything short of the rage of hunger should have
induced men to bear the misery of being the associates of the
Great King. It was no lucrative post. His Majesty was as
severe and economical in his friendships as in the other
5 charges of his establishment, and as unlikely to give a rixdollar too much for his guests as for his dinners. The sum
which he allowed to a poet or a philosopher was the very
smallest sum for which such poet or philosopher could be induced to sell himself into slavery ; and the bondsman might
10 think himself fortunate if what had been so grudgingly given
was not, after years of suffering, rudely and arbitrarily with-
drawn.

Potsdam was, in truth, what it was called by one of its
most illustrious inmates, the Palace of Alcina. At the first
15 glance it seemed to be a delightful spot, where every intellectual and physical enjoyment awaited the happy adventurer.
Every new-comer was received with eager hospitality, intoxi-
cated with flattery, encouraged to expect prosperity and greatness. It was in vain that a long succession of favorites who
20 had entered that abode with delight and hope, and who, after
a short term of delusive happiness, had been doomed to expiate
their folly by years of wretchedness and degradation, raised
their voices to warn the aspirant who approached the charmed
threshold. Some had wisdom enough to discover the truth
25 early, and spirit enough to fly without looking back ; others
lingered on to a cheerless and unhonored old age. We have
no hesitation in saying that the poorest author of that time in
London, sleeping on a bulk, dining in a cellar, with a cravat
of paper, and a skewer for a shirt-pin, was a happier man
30 than any of the literary inmates of Frederic's court.

But of all who entered the enchanted garden in the inebria-
tion of delight, and quitted it in agonies of rage and shame,
the most remarkable was Voltaire. Many circumstances had
made him desirous of finding a home at a distance from his

---

14. **Palace of Alcina.** In Ariosto's *Orlando Furioso*. Alcina is a kind
of Circe whose palace is a scene of enchantment. Alcina enjoys her lovers
for a season and then converts them into trees, stones, or wild beasts, as her
fancy dictates.

country. His fame had raised him up enemies. His sensibility gave them a formidable advantage over him. They were, indeed, contemptible assailants. Of all that they wrote against him, nothing has survived except what he has himself preserved. But the constitution of his mind resembled the 5 constitution of those bodies in which the slightest scratch of a bramble, or the bite of a gnat, never fails to fester. Though his reputation was rather raised than lowered by the abuse of such writers as Fréron and Desfontaines, though the vengeance which he took on Fréron and Desfontaines was such that 10 scourging, branding, pillorying would have been a trifle to it, there is reason to believe that they gave him far more pain than he ever gave them. Though he enjoyed during his own lifetime the reputation of a classic, though he was extolled by his contemporaries above all poets, philosophers, and historians, 15 though his works were read with as much delight and admiration at Moscow and Westminster, at Florence and Stockholm, as at Paris itself, he was yet tormented by that restless jealousy which should seem to belong only to minds burning with the desire of fame, and yet conscious of impotence. To men 20 of letters who could by no possibility be his rivals, he was, if they behaved well to him, not merely just, not merely courteous, but often a hearty friend and a munificent benefactor. But to every writer who rose to a celebrity approaching his own, he became either a disguised or an avowed enemy. He 25 slily depreciated Montesquieu and Buffon. He publicly, and with violent outrage, made war on Rousseau. Nor had he

9. **Freron and Desfontaines.** The editors of a critical review published in the first part of the eighteenth century.

26. **Charles de Secondat, Baron de Montesquieu** (1689–1755). A brilliant, original, and popular French author. He made deep researches into the labyrinths of history and political science. In respect to one of his works Voltaire said : "The human race lost its titles; Montesquieu found and restored them."

26. **Georges Louis Leclerc, Comte de Buffon** (1707–1788). An illustrious French naturalist and philosopher. He made many important discoveries in the realms of physical science and natural history. He tested by experiments the probability of the statement that Archimedes set fire to the Roman fleet by burning-mirrors, and succeeded in igniting wood at the distance of two hundred feet.

26. **Jean Jacques Rousseau** (1712–1778). A celebrated Swiss philosopher and writer. His early career presents a series of bizarre adventures, absurd vagaries, and surprising vicissitudes, of which he gave an extremely

the art of hiding his feelings under the semblance of good
humor or of contempt. With all his great talents, and all his
long experience of the world, he had no more self-command
than a petted child or a hysterical woman. Whenever he was
5 mortified, he exhausted the whole rhetoric of anger and sorrow
to express his mortification. His torrents of bitter words, his
stamping and cursing, his grimaces and his tears of rage, were
a rich feast to those abject natures whose delight is in the
agonies of powerful spirits and in the abasement of immortal
10 names. These creatures had now found out a way of galling
him to the very quick. In one walk, at least, it had been admitted by envy itself that he was without a living competitor.
Since Racine had been laid among the great men whose dust
made the holy precinct of Port Royal holier, no tragic poet had
15 appeared who could contest the palm with the author of Zaire,
of Alzire, and of Merope. At length a rival was announced.
Old Crébillon, who, many years before, had obtained some
theatrical success, and who had long been forgotten, came
forth from his garret in one of the meanest lanes near the
20 Rue St. Antoine, and was welcomed by the acclamations of
envious men of letters, and of a capricious populace. A
thing called *Catiline*, which he had written in his retirement,
was acted with boundless applause. Of this execrable piece
it is sufficient to say, that the plot turns on a love affair,
25 carried on in all the forms of Scudéry, between Catiline, whose
confidant is the Prætor Lentulus, and Tullia, the daughter of
Cicero. The theater resounded with acclamations. The king

---

candid and unreserved account in his *Confessions*. He produced in 1753 the
Discourse on the Origin of Inequality among Men, in which he maintains
that all men are born with equal rights. " He was the father of modern
democracy," says Professor Lowell, "and without him our Declaration of
Independence would have wanted some of those sentences in which the
immemorial longings of the poor, and the dreams of solitary enthusiasts
were at last affirmed in the manifesto of a nation, so that all the world
might hear."

15. **The author of Zaire, Alzire**, and of Merope—Voltaire.

17. **Crebillon**. Crebillon had enjoyed a great reputation as a tragic
writer before Voltaire's day.

25. **The forms of Scudéry**. Mlle. de Scudéry (1607–1701) was the leading member of that portion of French society which Molière satirizes in his
Précieuses Ridicules. She led a movement similar to the English *Euphuism*
of Elizabethan times, so well portrayed in Charles Kingsley's delightful
Westward Ho.

pensioned the successful poet; and the coffeehouses pronounced that Voltaire was a clever man, but that the real tragic inspiration, the celestial fire which had glowed in Corneille and Racine, was to be found in Crébillon alone.

The blow went to Voltaire's heart. Had his wisdom and 5 fortitude been in proportion to the fertility of his intellect, and to the brilliancy of his wit, he would have seen that it was out of the power of all the puffers and detractors in Europe to put Catiline above Zaire ; but he had none of the magnanimous patience with which Milton and Bentley left 10 their claims to the unerring judgment of time. He eagerly engaged in an undignified competition with Crébillon, and produced a series of plays on the same subjects which his rival had treated. These pieces were coolly received. Angry with the court, angry with the capital, Voltaire began to find 15 pleasure in the prospect of exile. His attachment for Madame du Châtelet long prevented him from executing his purpose. Her death set him at liberty, and he determined to take refuge at Berlin.

To Berlin he was invited by a series of letters, couched in 20 terms of the most enthusiastic friendship and admiration. For once the rigid parsimony of Frederic seemed to have relaxed. Orders, honorable offices, a liberal pension, a well-served table, stately apartments under a royal roof, were offered in return for the pleasure and honor which were ex- 25 pected from the society of the first wit of the age. A thousand louis were remitted for the charges of the journey. No am-

---

4. **Pierre Corneille** (1606–1684). A great French dramatic author, the founder of the French drama, and the writer who has perhaps contributed most to the development of the French national genius. Among his greatest works are *Le Cid, Cinna,* and *Polyeucte.*"

10. **John Milton** (1608–1674). An immortal poet, and if we except Shakespeare, the most illustrious name in English literature. His greatest works are the poems *Paradise Lost, Samson Agonistes, Paradise Regained, Lycidas, L'Allegro, Il Penseroso, Comus,* and the *Areopagitica,* a plea in prose for unlicensed printing.

10. **Richard Bentley** (1662–1742). A celebrated critic, regarded as the greatest classical scholar that England ever produced. His works are : *Latin Epistle to John Null,* two *Dissertations on the Epistle of Phalaris.* The Epistle of Phalaris was a forged letter from Christ to Phalaris, tyrant of Agrigentum, published by John Boyle. Bentley showed that this was a forgery. This gave rise to the first great English literary controversy.

bassador setting out from Berlin for a court of the first rank
had ever been more amply supplied. But Voltaire was not
satisfied. At a later period, when he possessed an ample fortune, he was one of the most liberal of men; but till his
5 means had become equal to his wishes, his greediness for lucre
was unrestrained either by justice or by shame. He had the
effrontery to ask for a thousand louis more, in order to enable
him to bring his niece, Madame Denis, the ugliest of coquettes,
in his company. The indelicate rapacity of the poet produced
10 its natural effect on the severe and frugal King. The answer
was a dry refusal. "I did not," said his Majesty, "solicit
the honor of the lady's society." On this, Voltaire went off
into a paroxysm of childish rage. "Was there ever such
avarice ! He has hundreds of tubs full of dollars in his vaults,
15 and haggles with me about a poor thousand louis." It seemed
that the negotiation would be broken off; but Frederic, with
great dexterity, affected indifference, and seemed inclined to
transfer his idolatry to Baculard D'Arnaud. His Majesty even
wrote some bad verses, of which the sense was, that Voltaire
20 was a setting sun, and that Arnaud was rising. Good-natured
friends soon carried the lines to Voltaire. He was in his bed.
He jumped out in his shirt, danced about the room with rage,
and sent for his passport and his post-horses. It was not
difficult to foresee the end of a connection which had such a
25 beginning.

It was in the year 1750 that Voltaire left the great capital,
which he was not to see again till, after the lapse of near
thirty years, he returned, bowed down by extreme old age, to
die in the midst of a splendid and ghastly triumph. His re-
30 ception in Prussia was such as might well have elated a less
vain and excitable mind. He wrote to his friends at Paris,
that the kindness and the attention with which he had been
welcomed surpassed description, that the King was the most
amiable of men, that Potsdam was the paradise of philoso-

---

18. **D'Arnaud.** A voluminous writer of plays, novels, etc. He is chiefly
famous for the reply he made to Frederick's question concerning Atheism :
"I rejoice to believe in the existence of a Being greater and wiser than
kings."

phers. He was created chamberlain, and received, together
with his gold key, the cross of an order, and a patent insuring
to him a pension of eight hundred pounds sterling a year for
life. A hundred and sixty pounds a year were promised to
his niece if she survived him. The royal cooks and coachmen 5
were put at his disposal. He was lodged in the same apartments in which Saxe had lived, when, at the height of power
and glory, he visited Prussia. Frederic, indeed, stooped for a
time even to use the language of adulation. He pressed to his
lips the meager hand of the little grinning skeleton, whom he 10
regarded as the dispenser of immortal renown. He would
add, he said, to the titles which he owed to his ancestors and
his sword, another title, derived from his last and proudest
acquisition. His style should run thus :—Frederic, King of
Prussia, Margrave of Brandenburg, Sovereign Duke of Silesia, 15
Possessor of Voltaire. But even amidst the delights of the
honeymoon, Voltaire's sensitive vanity began to take alarm.
A few days after his arrival, he could not help telling his
niece that the amiable King had a trick of giving a sly scratch
with one hand, while patting and stroking with the other. 20
Soon came hints not the less alarming, because mysterious.
" The supper parties are delicious. The King is the life of the
company. But—I have operas and comedies, reviews and
concerts, my studies and books. But—but—Berlin is fine, the
princesses charming, the maids of honor handsome. But "— 25
This eccentric friendship was fast cooling. Never had there
met two persons so exquisitely fitted to plague each other.
Each of them had exactly the fault of which the other was
most impatient ; and they were, in different ways, the most
impatient of mankind. Frederic was frugal, almost niggardly. 30
When he had secured his plaything, he began to think that he
had bought it too dear. Voltaire, on the other hand, was
greedy, even to the extent of impudence and knavery ; and
conceived that the favorite of a monarch, who had barrels full
of gold and silver laid up in cellars, ought to make a fortune 35
which a receiver-general might envy. They soon discovered
each other's feelings. Both were angry ; and a war began, in

which Frederic stooped to the part of Harpagon, and Voltaire
to that of Scapin. It is humiliating to relate, that the great
warrior and statesman gave orders that his guest's allowance
of sugar and chocolate should be curtailed. It is, if possible,
5 a still more humiliating fact, that Voltaire indemnified himself by pocketing the wax candles in the royal antechamber.
Disputes about money, however, were not the most serious
disputes of these extraordinary associates. The sarcasms of
the King soon galled the sensitive temper of the poet.
10 D'Arnaud and D'Argens, Guichard and La Métrie, might, for
the sake of a morsel of bread, be willing to bear the insolence
of a master ; but Voltaire was of another order. He knew
that he was a potentate as well as Frederic, that his European
reputation, and his incomparable power of covering whatever
15 he hated with ridicule, made him an object of dread even to
the leaders of armies and the rulers of nations. In truth, of
all the intellectual weapons which have ever been wielded by
man, the most terrible was the mockery of Voltaire. Bigots
and tyrants, who had never been moved by the wailing and
20 cursing of millions, turned pale at his name. Principles un-
assailable by reason, principles which had withstood the
fiercest attacks of power, the most valuable truths, the most
generous sentiments, the noblest and most graceful images,
the purest reputations, the most august institutions, began to
25 look mean and loathsome as soon as that withering smile was
turned upon them. To every opponent, however strong in his
cause and his talents, in his station and his character, who
ventured to encounter the great scoffer, might be addressed
the caution which was given of old to the Archangel :

30   " I forewarn thee shun
            His deadly arrow ; neither vainly hope
            To be invulnerable in those bright arms,
            Though temper'd heavenly ; for that fatal dint,
            Save Him who reigns above, none can resist."

---

  1. **Harpagon.** Harpagon, the avaricious old miser, is the leading character in Molière's comedy *L'Avare.*
  2. **Scapin.** A valet in Molière's comedy *Les Fourberies de Scapin.*
  10. **Guichard, La Metrie.** Minor French dramatic poets.
  30. From Milton's *Paradise Lost.*

We cannot pause to recount how often that rare talent was
exercised against rivals worthy of esteem ; how often it was
used to crush and torture enemies worthy only of silent dis-
dain ; how often it was perverted to the more noxious purpose
of destroying the last solace of earthly misery, and the last 5
restraint on earthly power.   Neither can we pause to tell how
often it was used to vindicate justice, humanity, and toleration, the principles of sound philosophy, the principles of free
government.   This is not the place for a full character of
Voltaire.   10

Causes of quarrel multiplied fast.   Voltaire, who, partly
from love of money, and partly from love of excitement, was
always fond of stockjobbing, became implicated in transactions
of at least a dubious character.   The King was delighted at
having such an opportunity to humble his guest ; and bitter 15
reproaches and complaints were exchanged.   Voltaire, too,
was soon at war with the other men of letters who surrounded
the King ; and this irritated Frederic, who, however, had
himself chiefly to blame : for, from that love of tormenting
which was in him a ruling passion, he perpetually lavished 20
extravagant praises on small men and bad books, merely in
order that he might enjoy the mortification and rage which on
such occasions Voltaire took no pains to conceal.   His majesty,
however, soon had reason to regret the pains which he had
taken to kindle jealousy among the members of his household. 25
The whole palace was in a ferment with literary intrigues and
cabals.   It was to no purpose that the imperial voice, which
kept a hundred and sixty thousand soldiers in order, was
raised to quiet the contention of the exasperated wits.   It
was far easier to stir up such a storm than to lull it.   Nor was 30
Frederic, in his capacity of wit, by any means without his own
share of vexations.   He had sent a large quantity of verses to
Voltaire, and requested that they might be returned, with re-
marks and corrections.   "See," exclaimed Voltaire, " what a
quantity of his dirty linen the King has sent me to wash !" 35

---

27. **Cabals.**   A cabal is a design secretly carried out by a small body of
men.

Tale-bearers were not wanting to carry the sarcasm to the royal ear; and Frederic was as much incensed as a Grub Street writer who had found his name in the Dunciad.

This could not last. A circumstance which, when the mutual regard of the friends was in its first glow, would merely have been matter for laughter, produced a violent explosion. Maupertuis enjoyed as much of Frederic's good-will as any man of letters. He was President of the Academy of Berlin; and he stood second to Voltaire, though at an immense distance, in the literary society which had been assembled at the Prussian court. Frederic had, by playing for his own amusement on the feelings of the two jealous and vainglorious Frenchmen, succeeded in producing a bitter enmity between them. Voltaire resolved to set his mark, a mark never to be effaced, on the forehead of Maupertuis, and wrote the exquisitely ludicrous Diatribe of Doctor Akakia. He showed this little piece to Frederic, who had too much taste and too much malice not to relish such delicious pleasantry. In truth, even at this time of day, it is not easy for any person who has the least perception of the ridiculous to read the jokes on the Latin city, the Patagonians, and the hole to the center of the earth, without laughing till he cries. But though Frederic was diverted by this charming pasquinade, he was unwilling that it shou'd get abroad. His self-love was interested. He had selected Maupertuis to fill the chair of his Academy. If all Europe were taught to laugh at Maupertuis, would not the reputation of the Academy, would not even the dignity of its royal patron, be in some degree compromised? The King, therefore, begged Voltaire to suppress this performance. Voltaire promised to do so, and broke his word. The Diatribe was published, and received with shouts of merriment and applause .

---

2. **Grub Street.** A street in London inhabited by literary hacks and poverty-stricken authors.

3. **Dunciad.** A satire by Alexander Pope, written to revenge himself upon his literary enemies.

23. **Pasquinade.** A kind of joke or lampoon at the expense of one's enemy was called a pasquinade. The word is derived from the name of a sixteenth-century Roman cobbler, whose shop was noted as a favorite resort for scandal-mongers.

by all who could read the French language. The King stormed.
Voltaire, with his usual disregard of truth, asserted his innocence, and made up some lie about a printer or an amanuensis.
The King was not to be so imposed upon. He ordered the
pamphlet to be burned by the common hangman, and insisted 5
upon having an apology from Voltaire, couched in the most
abject terms. Voltaire sent back to the King his cross, his
key, and the patent of his pension. After this burst of rage,
the strange pair began to be ashamed of their violence, and
went through the forms of reconciliation. But the breach was 10
irreparable ; and Voltaire took his leave of Frederic forever.
They parted with cold civility ; but their hearts were big with
resentment. Voltaire had in his keeping a volume of the
King's poetry, and forgot to return it. This was, we believe,
merely one of the oversights which men setting out upon a 15
journey often commit. That Voltaire could have meditated
plagiarism is quite incredible. He would not, we are confident, for the half of Frederic's kingdom, have consented to
father Frederic's verses. The King, however, who rated his
own writings much above their value, and who was inclined 20
to see all Voltaire's actions in the worst light, was enraged to
think that his favorite compositions were in the hands of an
enemy, as thievish as a daw and as mischievous as a monkey.
In the anger excited by this thought, he lost sight of reason
and decency, and determined on committing an outrage at 25
once odious and ridiculous.

Voltaire had reached Frankfort. His niece, Madame Denis,
came thither to meet him. He conceived himself secure from
the power of his late master, when he was arrested by order
of the Prussian resident. The precious volume was delivered 30
up. But the Prussian agents had, no doubt, been instructed
not to let Voltaire escape without some gross indignity. He
was confined twelve days in a wretched hovel. Sentinels with
fixed bayonets kept guard over him. His niece was dragged
through the mire by the soldiers. Sixteen hundred dollars 35

---

7. **Cross, key, patent.** See p. 59, l. 2.

were extorted from him by his insolent jailers. It is absurd
to say that this outrage is not to be attributed to the King.
Was anybody punished for it? Was anybody called in question for it? Was it not consistent with Frederic's character?
5 Was it not of a piece with his conduct on other similar occasions? Is it not notorious that he repeatedly gave private
directions to his officers to pillage and demolish the houses of
persons against whom he had a grudge, charging them at the
same time to take their measures in such a way that his name
10 might not be compromised? He acted thus towards Count
Bruhl in the Seven Years' War. Why should we believe that
he would have been more scrupulous with regard to Voltaire?

When at length the illustrious prisoner regained his liberty,
the prospect before him was but dreary. He was an exile both
15 from the country of his birth and from the country of his
adoption. The French government had taken offense at his
journey to Prussia, and would not permit him to return to
Paris ; and in the vicinity of Prussia it was not safe for him
to remain.

20   He took refuge on the beautiful shores of Lake Leman.
There, loosed from every tie which had hitherto restrained
him, and having little to hope or to fear from courts and
churches, he began his long war against all that, whether for
good or evil, had authority over man ; for what Burke said of
25 the Constituent Assembly, was eminently true of this its great
forerunner :—Voltaire could not build : he could only pull
down : he was the very Vitruvius of ruin. He has bequeathed
to us not a single doctrine to be called by his name, not a
single addition to the stock of our positive knowledge. But no
30 human teacher ever left behind him so vast and terrible a

---

24. **Edmund Burke** (1730–1797). One of England's greatest statesmen
and orators. Burke was a notably liberal-minded man, and spoke in favor
of the independence of the American colonies, while at the same time vio-
lently opposing the French Revolution. His speeches are marvels of English prose, but it is said that most of them were delivered in the House of
Commons before empty benches.
27. **Vitruvius.** A celebrated Roman architect and writer, about whom
very little is known. He served as a military engineer in his youth, and
was employed under Julius Cæsar in Africa in B.C. 46. His only work, *De
Architectura*, has been translated into English, and is the only ancient book
on architecture in existence.

wreck of truths and falsehoods, of things noble and things base, of things useful and things pernicious. From the time when his sojourn beneath the Alps commenced, the dramatist, the wit, the historian, was merged in a more important character. He was now the patriarch, the founder of a sect, 5 the chief of a conspiracy, the prince of a wide intellectual commonwealth. He often enjoyed a pleasure dear to the better part of his nature, the pleasure of vindicating innocence which had no other helper, of repairing cruel wrongs, of punishing tyranny in high places. He had also the satisfaction, 10 not less acceptable to his ravenous vanity, of hearing terrified Capuchins call him the Antichrist. But whether employed in works of benevolence, or in works of mischief, he never forgot Potsdam and Frankfort; and he listened anxiously to every murmur which indicated that a tempest was gathering in 15 Europe, and that his vengeance was at hand.

He soon had his wish. Maria Theresa had never for a moment forgotten the great wrong which she had received at the hand of Frederic. Young and delicate, just left an orphan, just about to be a mother, she had been compelled to fly 20 from the ancient capital of her race; she had seen her fair inheritance dismembered by robbers, and of those robbers he had been the foremost. Without a pretext, without a provocation, in defiance of the most sacred engagements, he had attacked the helpless ally whom he was bound to defend. The 25 Empress Queen had the faults as well as the virtues which are connected with quick sensibility and a high spirit. There was no peril which she was not ready to brave, no calamity which she was not ready to bring on her subjects, or on the whole human race, if only she might once taste the sweetness of a 30 complete revenge. Revenge, too, presented itself, to her narrow and superstitious mind, in the guise of duty. Silesia had been wrested not only from the House of Austria, but from the Church of Rome. The conqueror had indeed per-

---

12. **Capuchins.** The Capuchins were a religious order founded in 1525 by Matteo Baschi. They were an offshoot from the great Franciscan order. The name Capuchin comes from the fact that the monks were required to wear hoods or capuches.

mitted his new subjects to worship God after their own fashion; but this was not enough. To bigotry it seemed an intolerable hardship that the Catholic Church, having long enjoyed ascendency, should be compelled to content itself with 5 equality. Nor was this the only circumstance which led Maria Theresa to regard her enemy as the enemy of God. The profaneness of Frederic's writings and conversation, and the frightful rumors which were circulated respecting the immorality of his private life, naturally shocked a woman who 10 believed with the firmest faith all that her confessor told her, and who, though surrounded by temptations, though young and beautiful, though ardent in all her passions, though possessed of absolute power, had preserved her fame unsullied even by the breath of slander.

15 To recover Silesia, to humble the dynasty of Hohenzollern to the dust, was the great object of her life. She toiled during many years for this end, with zeal as indefatigable as that which the poet ascribes to the stately goddess who tired out her immortal horses in the work of raising the nations against 20 Troy, and who offered to give up to destruction her darling Sparta and Mycenæ, if only she might once see the smoke going up from the palace of Priam. With even such a spirit did the proud Austrian Juno strive to array against her foe a coalition such as Europe had never seen. Nothing would con- 25 tent her but that the whole civilized world, from the White Sea to the Adriatic, from the Bay of Biscay to the pastures of the wild horses of the Tanais, should be combined in arms against one petty state.

She early succeeded by various arts in obtaining the adhesion 30 of Russia. An ample share of spoil was promised to the King of Poland ; and that prince, governed by his favorite, Count Bruhl, readily promised the assistance of the Saxon forces. The great difficulty was with France. That the Houses of Bourbon and of Hapsburg should ever cordially co-operate in any 35 great scheme of European policy, had long been thought, to use

---

18. **Goddess.** Juno.

the strong expression of Frederic, just as impossible as that fire and water should amalgamate. The whole history of the Continent, during two centuries and a half, had been the history of the mutual jealousies and enmities of France and Austria. Since the administration of Richelieu, above all, it had been 5 considered as the plain policy of the Most Christian King to thwart on all occasions the Court of Vienna, and to protect every member of the Germanic body who stood up against the dictation of the Cæsars. Common sentiments of religion had been unable to mitigate this strong antipathy. The rulers of 10 France, even while clothed in the Roman purple, even while persecuting the heretics of Rochelle and Auvergne, had still looked with favor on the Lutheran and Calvinistic princes who were struggling against the chief of the empire. If the French ministers paid any respect to the traditional rules 15 handed down to them through many generations, they would have acted towards Frederic as the greatest of their predecessors acted towards Gustavus Adolphus. That there was deadly enmity between Prussia and Austria was of itself a sufficient reason for close friendship between Prussia and 20 France. With France Frederic could never have any serious controversy. His territories were so situated that his ambition, greedy and unscrupulous as it was, could never impel him to attack her of his own accord. He was more than half a Frenchman : he wrote, spoke, read nothing but French : he 25 delighted in French society : the admiration of the French he proposed to himself as the best reward of all his exploits. It seemed incredible that any French government, however notorious for levity or stupidity, could spurn away such an ally.

The Court of Vienna, however, did not despair. The Aus- 30

12. **Heretics.** The French Huguenots were persecuted in the most brutal ways. During the reign of Louis XIV., for instance, dragoons were posted in the houses of the Huguenots, with full permission to be as abusive as they wished.

17. **The greatest of their predecessors.** Richelieu.

18. **Gustavus Adolphus** (1594–1632). King of Sweden. During the Thirty Years' War he received a petition from the persecuted German Protestants to be the champion of their cause. He landed in Pomerania, and at once plunged into the conflict. Richelieu, prime-minister of France, helped him with provisions, ammunition, etc.

trian diplomatists propounded a new scheme of politics, which,
it must be owned, was not altogether without plausibility.
The great powers, according to this theory, had long been
under a delusion. They had looked on each other as natural
5 enemies, while in truth they were natural allies. A succession
of cruel wars had devastated Europe, had thinned the population, had exhausted the public resources, had loaded governments with an immense burden of debt ; and when, after two
hundred years of murderous hostility or of hollow truce, the
10 illustrious Houses whose enmity had distracted the world sat
down to count their gains, to what did the real advantage on
either side amount ? Simply to this, that they had kept each
other from thriving. It was not the King of France, it was
not the Emperor, who had reaped the fruits of the Thirty
15 Years' War, or of the War of the Pragmatic Sanction. Those
fruits had been pilfered by states of the second and third rank,
which, secured against jealousy by their insignificance, had dex-
terously aggrandized themselves while pretending to serve the
animosity of the great chiefs of Christendom. While the lion
20 and tiger were tearing each other, the jackal had run off into
the jungle with the prey. The real gainer by the Thirty Years'
War had been neither France nor Austria, but Sweden. The
real gainer by the War of the Pragmatic Sanction had been
neither France nor Austria, but the upstart of Brandenburg.
25 France had made great efforts, had added largely to her military glory, and largely to her public burdens ; and for what
end ? Merely that Frederic might rule Silesia. For this and
this alone one French army, wasted by sword and famine, had
perished in Bohemia ; and another had purchased, with floods
30 of the noblest blood, the barren glory of Fontenoy. And this
prince, for whom France had suffered so much, was he a grate-
ful, was he even an honest ally ? Had he not been as false to

---

14. **Thirty Years' War.** From 1618 until 1648 all Europe was aflame
with war. The war may be divided into two great periods. The first had a
predominant religious character. It was a general attack by Catholic Europe upon Protestant Europe. The second part was composed of political
wars—wars against the power of the House of Hapsburg, and wars of conquest on the part of Sweden and France on German soil.

the Court of Versailles as to the Court of Vienna ? Had he
not played, on a large scale, the same part which, in private
life, is played by the vile agent of chicane who sets his neighbors quarreling, involves them in costly and interminable
litigation, and betrays them to each other all round, certain 5
that, whoever may be ruined, he shall be enriched ?   Surely the
true wisdom of the great powers was to attack, not each other,
but this common barrator, who, by inflaming the passions of
both, by pretending to serve both, and by deserting both, had
raised himself above the station to which he was born.   The 10
great object of Austria was to regain Silesia ; the great object
of France was to obtain an accession of territory on the side of
Flanders.   If they took opposite sides, the result would probably be that, after a war of many years, after the slaughter of
many thousands of brave men, after the waste of many mil- 15
lions of crowns, they would lay down their arms without
having achieved either object ; but, if they came to an understanding, there would be no risk, and no difficulty.   Austria
would willingly make in Belgium such cessions as France
could not expect to obtain by ten pitched battles.   Silesia 20
would easily be annexed to the monarchy of which it had long
been a part.   The union of two such powerful governments
would at once overawe the King of Prussia.   If he resisted,
one short campaign would settle his fate.   France and Austria,
long accustomed to rise from the game of war both losers, 25
would, for the first time, both be gainers.   There could be no
room for jealousy between them.   The power of both would
be increased at once ; the equilibrium between them would be
preserved ; and the only sufferer would be a mischievous and
unprincipled buccaneer, who deserved no tenderness from 30
either.

These doctrines, attractive from their novelty and ingenuity,
soon became fashionable at the supper-parties and in the
coffeehouses of Paris, and were espoused by every gay marquis
and every facetious abbé who was admitted to see Madame de 35

---

8. **Barrator.**   One who stirs up quarrels, hoping to reap some benefit
from them for himself.

Pompadour's hair curled and powdered. It was not, however, to any political theory that the strange coalition between France and Austria owed its origin. The real motive which induced the great continental powers to forget their old ani-
5 mosities and their old state maxims, was personal aversion to the King of Prussia. This feeling was strongest in Maria Theresa ; but it was by no means confined to her. Frederic, in some respects a good master, was emphatically a bad neighbor. That he was hard in all dealings, and quick to take all ad-
10 vantages, was not his most odious fault. His bitter and scoffing speech had inflicted keener wounds than his ambition. In his character of wit he was under less restraint than even in his character of ruler. Satirical verses against all the princes and ministers of Europe were ascribed to his pen. In his letters
15 and conversation he alluded to the greatest potentates of the age in terms which would have better suited Collé, in a war of repartee with young Crébillon at Pelletier's table, than a great sovereign speaking of great sovereigns. About women he was in the habit of expressing himself in a manner which it was
20 impossible for the meekest of women to forgive ; and, unfortunately for him, almost the whole Continent was then governed by women who were by no means conspicuous for meekness. Maria Theresa herself had not escaped his scurrilous jests. The Empress Elizabeth of Russia knew that her gallan-
25 tries afforded him a favorite theme for ribaldry and invective. Madame de Pompadour, who was really the head of the French government, had been even more keenly galled. She had attempted, by the most delicate flattery, to propitiate the King of Prussia ; but her messages had drawn from him only dry and sarcastic replies. The Empress Queen took a very
30 different course. Though the haughtiest of princesses, though the most austere of matrons, she forgot in her thirst for re-

---

1. **Madame de Pompadour** (1721-1764). A woman whose beauty and accomplishments obtained for her the signal favor of Louis XV. of France. She retained a dominant influence over him till her death. She appointed generals and ministers, and received ambassadors from foreign courts.
16. **Charles Collé** (1709 1783). A French comic writer who attained some success in his day.

venge both the dignity of her race and the purity of her character, and condescended to flattery. Maria Theresa actually wrote with her own hand a note, full of expressions of esteem and friendship, to her dear cousin, the daughter of the butcher Poisson, the wife of the publican D'Etioles, a strange cousin 5 for the descendant of so many Emperors of the West! Madame de Pompadour was completely gained over, and easily carried her point with Lewis, who had, indeed, wrongs of his own to resent. His feelings were not quick; but contempt, says the Eastern proverb, pierces even through the shell of the 10 tortoise; and neither prudence nor decorum had ever restrained Frederic from expressing his measureless contempt for the sloth, the imbecility, and the baseness of Lewis. France was thus induced to join the coalition; and the example of France determined the conduct of Sweden, then com- 15 pletely subject to French influence.

The enemies of Frederic were surely strong enough to attack him openly; but they were desirous to add to all their other advantages the advantage of a surprise. He was not, however, a man to be taken off his guard. He had tools in 20 every court; and he now received from Vienna, from Dresden, and from Paris, accounts so circumstantial and so consistent, that he could not doubt of his danger. He learnt, that he was to be assailed at once by France, Austria, Russia, Saxony, Sweden, and the Germanic body; that the greater part of his 25 dominions was to be portioned out among his enemies; that France, which from her geographical position could not directly share in his spoils, was to receive an equivalent in the Netherlands; that Austria was to have Silesia, and the Czarina East Prussia; that Augustus of Saxony expected 30 Magdeburg; and that Sweden would be rewarded with part of Pomerania. If these designs succeeded, the house of Brandenburg would at once sink in the European system to a place lower than that of the Duke of Wurtemburg or the Margrave of Baden. 35

And what hope was there that these designs would fail? No such union of the continental powers had been seen for

ages. A less formidable confederacy had in a week conquered
all the provinces of Venice, when Venice was at the height of
power, wealth, and glory. A less formidable confederacy had
compelled Lewis the Fourteenth to bow down his haughty
5 head to the very earth. A less formidable confederacy has,
within our own memory, subjugated a still mightier empire,
and abased a still prouder name. Such odds had never been
heard of in war. The people whom Frederic ruled were not
five millions. The population of the countries which were
10 leagued against him amounted to a hundred millions. The
disproportion in wealth was at least equally great. Small
communities, actuated by strong sentiments of patriotism or
loyalty, have sometimes made head against great monarchies
weakened by factions and discontents. But, small as was
15 Frederic's kingdom, it probably contained a greater number
of disaffected subjects than were to be found in all the states
of his enemies. Silesia formed a fourth part of his dominions ;
and from the Silesians, born under Austrian princes, the
utmost that he could expect was apathy. From the Silesian
20 Catholics he could hardly expect anything but resistance.

Some states have been enabled, by their geographical position, to defend themselves with advantage against immerse
force. The sea has repeatedly protected England against the
fury of the whole continent. The Venetian government,
25 driven from its possessions on the land, could still bid defiance
to the confederates of Cambray from the Arsenal amidst the
lagoons. More than one great and well-appointed army,
which regarded the shepherds of Switzerland as an easy prey,
has perished in the passes of the Alps. Frederic had no such
30 advantage. The form of his states, their situation, the nature
of the ground, all were against him. His long, scattered,
straggling territory, seemed to have been shaped with an
express view to the convenience of invaders, and was protected
by no sea, by no chain of hills. Scarcely any corner of it was

___

6. **A still mightier empire.** In 1815 at the battle of Waterloo the
Emperor Napoleon was utterly defeated by the English under Wellington,
assisted by the allied powers of Europe.

a week's march from the territory of the enemy. The capital itself, in the event of war, would be constantly exposed to insult. In truth there was hardly a politician or a soldier in Europe who doubted that the conflict would be terminated in a very few days by the prostration of the House of Branden- 5 burg.

Nor was Frederic's own opinion very different. He anticipated nothing short of his own ruin, and of the ruin of his family. Yet there was still a chance, a slender chance, of escape. His states had at least the advantage of a central 10 position ; his enemies were widely separated from each other, and could not conveniently unite their overwhelming forces on one point. They inhabited different climates, and it was probable that the season of the year which would be best suited to the military operations of one portion of the league 15 would be unfavorable to those of another portion. The Prussian monarchy, too, was free from some infirmities which were found in empires far more extensive and magnificent. Its effective strength for a desperate struggle was not to be measured merely by the number of square miles or the number 20 of people. In that spare but well-knit and well-exercised body there was nothing but sinew, and muscle, and bone. No public creditors looked for dividends. No distant colonies required defense. No court, filled with flatterers and mistresses, devoured the pay of fifty battalions. The Prussian 25 army, though far inferior in number to the troops which were about to be opposed to it, was yet strong out of all proportion to the extent of the Prussian dominions. It was also admirably trained and admirably officered, accustomed to obey and accustomed to conquer. The revenue was not only unincum- 30 bered by debt, but exceeded the ordinary outlay in time of peace. Alone of all the European princes, Frederic had a treasure laid up for a day of difficulty. Above all, he was one, and his enemies were many. In their camps would certainly be found the jealousy, the dissension, the slackness, insepara- 35 ble from coalitions ; on his side was the energy, the unity, the secrecy of a strong dictatorship. To a certain extent the de-

ficiency of military means might be supplied by the resources
of military art. Small as the King's army was, when compared with the six hundred thousand men whom the confederates could bring into the field, celerity of movement might
5 in some degree compensate for deficiency of bulk. It was
thus just possible that genius, judgment, resolution, and good-
luck united, might protract the struggle during a campaign or
two ; and to gain even a month was of importance. It could
not be long before the vices which are found in all extensive
10 confederacies would begin to show themselves. Every member of the league would think his own share of the war too
large, and his own share of the spoils too small. Complaints
and recriminations would abound. The Turk might stir on
the Danube ; the statesmen of France might discover the error
15 which they had committed in abandoning the fundamental
principles of their national policy. Above all, death might
rid Prussia of its most formidable enemies. The war was the
effect of the personal aversion with which three or four sovereigns regarded Frederic ; and the decease of any one of those
20 sovereigns might produce a complete revolution in the state of
Europe.

In the midst of a horizon generally dark and stormy, Frederic could discern one bright spot. The peace which had been
concluded between England and France in 1748 had been in
25 Europe no more than an armistice, and had not even been an
armistice in the other quarters of the globe. In India the
sovereignty of the Carnatic was disputed between two great
Mussulman houses ; Fort Saint George had taken one side,
Pondicherry the other ; and in a series of battles and sieges
30 the troops of Lawrence and Clive had been opposed to those of
Dupleix. A struggle less important in its consequences, but
not less likely to produce irritation, was carried on between
those French and English adventurers who kidnapped negroes
and collected gold-dust on the coast of Guinea. But it was in

---

27. **Carnatic.** A region on the east coast of India now included in the
province of Madras. The Carnatic is no longer an administrative division,
but is memorable as the theater of the struggle of last century between
France and England for supremacy in India.

North America that the emulation and mutual aversion of the two nations were most conspicuous. The French attempted to hem in the English colonists by a chain of military posts, extending from the Great Lakes to the mouth of the Mississippi. The English took arms. The wild aboriginal tribes appeared 5 on each side mingled with the Pale Faces. Battles were fought ; forts were stormed ; and hideous stories about stakes, scalpings, and death-songs reached Europe, and inflamed that national animosity which the rivalry of ages had produced. The disputes between France and England came to a crisis at 10 the very time when the tempest which had been gathering was about to burst on Prussia. The tastes and interests of Frederic would have led him, if he had been allowed an option, to side with the House of Bourbon. But the folly of the Court of Versailles left him no choice. France became the tool of 15 Austria ; and Frederic was forced to become the ally of England. He could not, indeed, expect that a power which covered the sea with its fleets, and which had to make war at once on the Ohio and the Ganges, would be able to spare a large number of troops for operations in Germany. But Eng- 20 land, though poor compared with the England of our time, was far richer than any country on the Continent. The amount of her revenue, and the resources which she found in her credit, though they may be thought small by a generation which has seen her raise a hundred and thirty millions in a 25 single year, appeared miraculous to the politicians of that age. A very moderate portion of her wealth, expended by an able and economical prince, in a country where prices were low, would be sufficient to equip and maintain a formidable army.

Such was the situation in which Frederic found himself. 30 He saw the whole extent of his peril. He saw that there was still a faint possibility of escape ; and, with prudent temerity, he determined to strike the first blow. It was in the month of August 1756, that the great war of the Seven Years commenced. The King demanded of the Empress Queen a dis- 35 tinct explanation of her intentions, and plainly told her that he should consider a refusal as a declaration of war. "I

want," he said, " no answer in the style of an oracle." He received an answer at once haughty and evasive. In an instant the rich electorate of Saxony was overflowed by sixty thousand Prussian troops. Augustus with his army occupied a strong
5 position at Pirna. The Queen of Poland was at Dresden. In a few days Pirna was blockaded and Dresden was taken. The first object of Frederic was to obtain possession of the Saxon State Papers ; for those papers, he well knew, contained ample proofs that, though apparently an aggressor, he was really
10 acting in self-defense. The Queen of Poland, as well acquainted as Frederic with the importance of those documents, had packed them up, had concealed them in her bed-chamber, and was about to send them off to Warsaw, when a Prussian officer made his appearance. In the hope that no soldier
15 would venture to outrage a lady, a queen, the daughter of an emperor, the mother-in-law of a dauphin, she placed herself before the trunk, and at length sat down on it. But all resistance was vain. The papers were carried to Frederic, who found in them, as he expected, abundant evidence of the de-
20 signs of the coalition. The most important documents were instantly published, and the effect of the publication was great. It was clear that, of whatever sins the King of Prussia might formerly have been guilty, he was now the injured party, and had merely anticipated a blow intended to destroy
25 him.

The Saxon camp at Pirna was in the mean time closely invested ; but the besieged were not without hopes of succor. A great Austrian army under Marshal Brown was about to pour through the passes which separate Bohemia from Saxony.
30 Frederic left at Pirna a force sufficient to deal with the Saxons, hastened into Bohemia, encountered Brown at Lowositz, and defeated him. This battle decided the fate of Saxony. Augustus and his favorite Bruhl fled to Poland.

---

4. **Frederic Augustus II.** (1696–1763). The Elector of Saxony and King of Poland.
28. **Maximilian Browne** (1705–1757). A famous general in the Austrian service. Frederic used to call him his teacher in the art of war.

The whole army of the electorate capitulated. From that time till the end of the war Frederic treated Saxony as a part of his dominions, or, rather, he acted towards the Saxons in a manner which may serve to illustrate the whole meaning of that tremendous sentence, " subjectos tanquam suos, viles 5 tanquam alienos." Saxony was as much in his power as Brandenburg ; and he had no such interest in the welfare of Saxony as he had in the welfare of Brandenburg. He accordingly levied troops and exacted contributions throughout the enslaved province with far more rigor than in any part of his 10 own dominions. Seventeen thousand men who had been in the camp at Pirna were half compelled, half persuaded to enlist under their conqueror. Thus, within a few weeks from the commencement of hostilities, one of the confederates had been disarmed, and his weapons were now pointed against the 15 rest.

The winter put a stop to military operations. All had hitherto gone well. But the real tug of war was still to come. It was easy to foresee that the year 1757 would be a memorable era in the history of Europe. 20

The King's scheme for the campaign was simple, bold, and judicious. The Duke of Cumberland with an English and Hanoverian army was in Western Germany, and might be able to prevent the French troops from attacking Prussia. The Russians, confined by their snows, would probably not 25 stir till the spring was far advanced. Saxony was prostrated. Sweden could do nothing very important. During a few months Frederic would have to deal with Austria alone. Even thus the odds were against him. But ability and courage have often triumphed against odds still more formidable. 30

Early in 1757 the Prussian army in Saxony began to move. Through four defiles in the mountains they came pouring into Bohemia. Prague was the King's first mark ; but the ulterior object was probably Vienna. At Prague lay Marshal Brown with one great army. Daun, the most cautious and fortunate 35

---

6. They were as much under his sway as were his own people, yet they were as little cared for as men of other nations would have been.

of the Austrian captains, was advancing with another. Frederic determined to overwhelm Brown before Daun should arrive. On the sixth of May was fought, under those walls which, a hundred and thirty years before, had witnessed the
5 victory of the Catholic league and the flight of the unhappy Palatine, a battle more bloody than any which Europe saw during the long interval between Malplaquet and Eylau. The King and Prince Ferdinand of Brunswick were distinguished on that day by their valor and exertions. But the chief glory
10 was with Schwerin. When the Prussian infantry wavered, the stout old marshal snatched the colors from an ensign, and, waving them in the air, led back his regiment to the charge. Thus at seventy-two years of age he fell in the thickest battle, still grasping the standard which bears the black eagle on
15 the field argent. The victory remained with the King ; but it had been dearly purchased. Whole columns of his bravest warriors had fallen. He admitted that he had lost eighteen thousand men. Of the enemy, twenty-four thousand had been killed, wounded, or taken.
20   Part of the defeated army was shut up in Prague. Part fled to join the troops which, under the command of Daun, were now close at hand. Frederic determined to play over the same game which had succeeded at Lowositz. He left a large force to besiege Prague, and at the head of thirty thou-
25 sand men he marched against Daun. The cautious Marshal, though he had a great superiority in numbers, would risk nothing. He occupied at Kolin a position almost impregnable, and awaited the attack of the King.

It was the eighteenth of June, a day which, if the Greek
30 superstition still retained its influence, would be held sacred to Nemesis, a day on which the two greatest princes of modern times were taught, by a terrible experience, that neither skill nor valor can fix the inconstancy of fortune. The battle began

---

31. **Greek superstition, Nemesis.** Nemesis, according to Hesiod, was the Greek personification of the moral feeling of right and a just horror of criminal actions : in other words, of the conscience. Afterwards Nemesis came to be regarded as the power who constantly preserves and restores the moral equilibrium of earthly affairs

before noon ; and part of the Prussian army maintained the contest till after the midsummer sun had gone down. But at length the King found that his troops, having been repeatedly driven back with frightful carnage, could no longer be led to the charge. He was with difficulty persuaded to quit the field. 5 The officers of his personal staff were under the necessity of expostulating with him, and one of them took the liberty to say, "Does your Majesty mean to storm the batteries alone?" Thirteen thousand of his bravest followers had perished. Nothing remained for him but to retreat in good order, to 10 raise the siege of Prague, and to hurry his army by different routes out of Bohemia.

This stroke seemed to be final. Frederic's situation had at best been such, that only an uninterrupted run of good-luck could save him, as it seemed, from ruin. And now, almost in 15 the outset of the contest, he had met with a check which, even in a war between equal powers, would have been felt as serious. He had owed much to the opinion which all Europe entertained of his army. Since his accession, his soldiers had in many successive battles been victorious over the Austrians. 20 But the glory had departed from his arms. All whom his malevolent sarcasms had wounded, made haste to avenge themselves by scoffing at the scoffer. His soldiers had ceased to confide in his star. In every part of his camp his dispositions were severely criticised. Even in his own family he had 25 detractors. His next brother William, heir-presumptive, or rather in truth heir-apparent, to the throne, and great-grandfather of the present King, could not refrain from lamenting his own fate and that of the House of Hohenzollern, once so great and so prosperous, but now, by the rash ambition of its 30 chief, made a by-word to all nations. These complaints, and some blunders which William committed during the retreat from Bohemia, called forth the bitter displeasure of the inexorable King. The prince's heart was broken by the cutting reproaches of his brother ; he quitted the army, retired to a 35 country-seat, and in a short time died of shame and vexation.

It seemed that the King's distress could hardly be increased.

Yet at this moment another blow not less terrible than that of Kolin fell upon him. The French under Marshal D'Estrées had invaded Germany. The Duke of Cumberland had given them battle at Hastembeck, and had been defeated. In order 5 to save the Electorate of Hanover from entire subjugation, he had made, at Closter Sevan, an arrangement with the French Generals, which left them at liberty to turn their arms against the Prussian dominions.

That nothing might be wanting to Frederic's distress, he 10 lost his mother just at this time ; and he appears to have felt the loss more than was to be expected from the hardness and severity of his character. In truth, his misfortunes had now cut to the quick. The mocker, the tyrant, the most rigorous, the most imperious, the most cynical of men, was very un- 15 happy. His face was so haggard and his form so thin, that when on his return from Bohemia he passed through Leipsic, the people hardly knew him again. His sleep was broken ; the tears, in spite of himself, often started into his eyes ; and the grave began to present itself to his agitated mind as the 20 best refuge from misery and dishonor. His resolution was fixed never to be taken alive, and never to make peace on condition of descending from his place among the powers of Europe. He saw nothing left for him except to die ; and he deliberately chose his mode of death. He always carried about 25 with him a sure and speedy poison in a small glass case ; and to the few in whom he placed confidence, he made no mystery of his resolution.

But we should very imperfectly describe the state of Frederic's mind, if we left out of view the laughable peculiarities 30 which contrasted so singularly with the gravity, energy, and harshness of his character. It is difficult to say whether the tragic or the comic predominated in the strange scene which was then acting. In the midst of all the great King's calamities, his passion for writing indifferent poetry grew stronger 35 and stronger. Enemies all round him, despair in his heart, pills of corrosive sublimate hidden in his clothes, he poured forth hundreds upon hundreds of lines, hateful to gods and

men, the insipid dregs of Voltaire's Hippocrene, the faint echo
of the lyre of Chaulieu. It is amusing to compare what he
did during the last months of 1757, with what he wrote during
the same time. It may be doubted whether any equal portion
of the life of Hannibal, of Cæsar, or of Napoleon, will bear a [5]
comparison with that short period, the most brilliant in the
history of Prussia and of Frederic. Yet at this very time the
scanty leisure of the illustrious warrior was employed in producing odes and epistles, a little better than Cibber's and a
little worse than Hayley's. Here and there a manly sentiment [10]
which deserves to be in prose makes its appearance in company with Prometheus and Orpheus, Elysium and Acheron,
the plaintive Philomel, the poppies of Morpheus, and all the
other frippery which, like a robe tossed by a proud beauty to
her waiting-woman, has long been contemptuously abandoned [15]
by genius to mediocrity. We hardly know any instance of the
strength and weakness of human nature so striking, and so
grotesque, as the character of this haughty, vigilant, resolute,
sagacious blue-stocking, half Mithridates and half Trissotin,

---

1. **Hippocrene.** The fountain of the Muses. Longfellow calls poetic
inspiration "a maddening draught of Hippocrene."

2. **Guillaume de Chaulieu** (1639-1720). A French lyric poet. Voltaire
praises him in his *Temple du Gout*, where he advises Chaulieu not to
estimate himself the best of good poets, but the first of negligent poets
(*poètes négligés*).

5. **Napoleon.** Napoleon was defeated at Waterloo June 18th.

9. **Colley Cibber** (1671-1757). A witty English dramatic author and
actor. He effected something of a reform in the English stage ; that is, he
tried to make it a little less vulgar, and though to our eyes his plays may
seem not over nice, yet as compared with what had been in vogue before
his time, they were perfectly refined.

Cibber wrote an amusing *Apology for the Life of Colley Cibber*, which
Dr. Johnson pronounced "very well done." Cibber is a prominent character in Pope's *Dunciad*.

10. **William Hayley** (1745-1820). An English author, not without taste,
but whose poetry is infected with mawkish sentimentality. Southey once
remarked, "Everything about that man is good except his poetry."

12. **Prometheus, Orpheus.** Prometheus, having stolen fire from heaven
for the benefit of man, was punished by being chained to a pillar while an
eagle tore out his heart. Orpheus was the musician on whose notes all
nature hung enchanted.

12. **Elysium, Acheron, Philomel, Morpheus.** In Greek mythology,
Elysium was the home of the good and brave after death. Acheron was
the river in Hades across which the dead were ferried by Charon. Philomel,
being pursued by her brother-in-law, who wished to kill her, was changed
into a nightingale. Morpheus was the Greek god of sleep.

19. **Trissotin.** In Molière's comedy, *Les Femmes Savantes*, Trissotin is a
character. He typifies the shallow wit of Molière's day.

bearing up against a world in arms, with an ounce of poison
in one pocket and a quire of bad verses in the other.

Frederick had some time before made advances towards a
reconciliation with Voltaire ; and some civil letters had passed
5 between them.   After the battle of Kolin their epistolary in-
tercourse became, at least in seeming, friendly and confiden-
tial.   We do not know any collection of Letters which throws
so much light on the darkest and most intricate parts of
human nature, as the correspondence of these strange beings
10 after they had exchanged forgiveness.   Both felt that the
quarrel had lowered them in the public estimation.   They admired each other.   They stood in need of each other.   The
great King wished to be handed down to posterity by the great
Writer.   The great Writer felt himself exalted by the homage
15 of the great King.   Yet the wounds which they had inflicted on each other were too deep to be effaced, or even perfectly healed.   Not only did the scars remain ; the sore places
often festered and bled afresh.   The letters consisted for the
most part of compliments, thanks, offers of service, assurances
20 of attachment.   But if anything brought back to Frederic's
recollection the cunning and mischievous pranks by which
Voltaire had provoked him, some expression of contempt and
displeasure broke forth in the midst of eulogy.   It was much
worse when anything recalled to the mind of Voltaire the out-
25 rages which he and his kinswoman had suffered at Frankfort.
All at once his flowing panegyric was turned into invective.
" Remember how you behaved to me.   For your sake I have
lost the favor of my native king.   For your sake I am an exile
from my country.   I loved you.   I trusted myself to you.   I
30 had no wish but to end my life in your service.   And what
was my reward ?   Stripped of all that you had bestowed on
me, the key, the order, the pension, I was forced to fly from
your territories.   I was hunted as if I had been a deserter
from your grenadiers.   I was arrested, insulted, plundered.
35 My niece was dragged through the mud of Frankfort by your
soldiers, as if she had been some wretched follower of your
camp.   You have great talents.   You have good qualities.

But you have one odious vice. You delight in the abasement of your fellow-creatures. You have brought disgrace on the name of philosopher. You have given some color to the slanders of the bigots, who say that no confidence can be placed in the justice or humanity of those who reject the Christian faith." Then the King answers, with less heat but equal severity: " You know that you behaved shamefully in Prussia. It was well for you that you had to deal with a man so indulgent to the infirmities of genius as I am. You richly deserved to see the inside of a dungeon. Your talents are not more widely known than your faithlessness and your malevolence. The grave itself is no asylum from your spite. Maupertuis is dead ; but you still go on calumniating and deriding him, as if you had not made him miserable enough while he was living. Let us have no more of this. And, above all, let me hear no more of your niece. I am sick to death of her name. I can bear with your faults for the sake of your merits ; but she has not written Mahomet or Merope."

An explosion of this kind, it might be supposed, would necessarily put an end to all amicable communication. But it was not so. After every outbreak of ill-humor this extraordinary pair became more loving than before, and exchanged compliments and assurances of mutual regard with a wonderful air of sincerity.

It may well be supposed that men who wrote thus to each other, were not very guarded in what they said of each other. The English ambassador, Mitchell, who knew that the King of Prussia was constantly writing to Voltaire with the greatest freedom on the most important subjects, was amazed to hear his Majesty designate this highly favored correspondent as a bad-hearted fellow, the greatest rascal on the face of the earth. And the language which the poet held about the King was not much more respectful.

It would probably have puzzled Voltaire himself to say what was his real feeling towards Frederic. It was compounded of all sentiments, from enmity to friendship, and from scorn to admiration ; and the proportions in which these elements were

mixed, changed every moment. The old patriarch resembled
the spoiled child who screams, stamps, cuffs, laughs, kisses,
and cuddles within one quarter of an hour. His resentment
was not extinguished ; yet he was not without sympathy for
5 his old friend. As a Frenchman, he wished success to the
arms of his country. As a philosopher, he was anxious for
the stability of a throne on which a philosopher sat. He
longed both to save and to humble Frederic. There was one
way, and only one, in which all his conflicting feelings could
10 at once be gratified. If Frederic were preserved by the interference of France, if it were known that for that interference
he was indebted to the mediation of Voltaire, this would indeed be delicious revenge ; this would indeed be to heap coals
of fire on that haughty head. Nor did the vain and restless
15 poet think it impossible that he might, from his hermitage
near the Alps, dictate peace to Europe. D'Estrées had quitted
Hanover, and the command of the French army had been intrusted to the Duke of Richelieu, a man whose chief distinction was derived from his success in gallantry. Richelieu was
20 in truth the most eminent of that race of seducers by profession, who furnished Crébillon the younger and La Clos with
models for their heroes. In his earlier days the royal house
itself had not been secure from his presumptuous love. He
was believed to have carried his Conquests into the family of
25 Orleans ; and some suspected that he was not unconcerned in
the mysterious remorse which embittered the last hours of the
charming mother of Lewis the Fifteenth. But the Duke was
now sixty years old. With a heart deeply corrupted by vice,
a head long accustomed to think only on trifles, an impaired
30 constitution, an impaired fortune, and, worst of all, a very
red nose, he was entering on a dull, frivolous, and unrespected
old age. Without one qualification for military command,
except that personal courage which was common between him
and the whole nobility of France, he had been placed at the

---

16. **D'Estrees.** A French field-marshal.
18. **Duke of Richelieu.** A grand nephew of the great Cardinal
Richelieu.

head of the army of Hanover ; and in that situation he did
his best to repair, by extortion and corruption, the injury
which he had done to his property, by a life of dissolute pro-
fusion.

The Duke of Richelieu to the end of his life hated the phi- 5
losophers as a sect, not for those parts of their system which
a good and wise man would have condemned, but for their
virtues, for their spirit of free inquiry, and for their hatred of
those social abuses of which he was himself the personification.
But he, like many of those who thought with him, excepted 10
Voltaire from the list of proscribed writers. He frequently
sent flattering letters to Ferney. He did the patriarch the
honor to borrow money of him, and even carried this conde-
scending friendship so far as to forget to pay the interest.
Voltaire thought that it might be in his power to bring the 15
Duke and the King of Prussia into communication with each
other. He wrote earnestly to both ; and he so far succeeded
that a correspondence between them was commenced.

But it was to very different means that Frederic was to owe
his deliverance. At the beginning of November, the net 20
seemed to have closed completely round him. The Russians
were in the field, and were spreading devastation through his
eastern provinces. Silesia was overrun by the Austrians. A
great French army was advancing from the west under the
command of Marshal Soubise, a prince of the great Armorican 25
house of Rohan. Berlin itself had been taken and plundered
by the Croatians. Such was the situation from which Frederic
extricated himself, with dazzling glory, in the short space of
thirty days.

He marched first against Soubise. On the fifth of Novem- 30
ber the armies met at Rosbach. The French were two to one ;
but they were ill-disciplined, and their general was a dunce.
The tactics of Frederic, and the well-regulated valor of the
Prussian troops, obtained a complete victory. Seven thousand
of the invaders were made prisoners. Their guns, their colors, 35

12. **Ferney.** Voltaire's home on Lake Geneva.

their baggage, fell into the hands of the conquerors. Those who escaped fled as confusedly as a mob scattered by cavalry. Victorious in the west, the King turned his arms towards Silesia. In that quarter everything seemed to be lost. Breslau had fallen ; and Charles of Loraine, with a mighty power, held the whole province. On the fifth of December, exactly one month after the battle of Rosbach, Frederic, with forty thousand men, and Prince Charles, at the head of not less than sixty thousand, met at Leuthen, hard by Breslau. The King, who was, in general, perhaps too much inclined to consider the common soldier as a mere machine, resorted, on this great day, to means resembling those which Bonaparte afterwards employed with such signal success for the purpose of stimulating military enthusiasm. The principal officers were convoked. Frederic addressed them with great force and pathos ; and directed them to speak to their men as he had spoken to them. When the armies were set in battle array, the Prussian troops were in a state of fierce excitement ; but their excitement showed itself after the fashion of a grave people. The columns advanced to the attack chanting, to the sound of drums and fifes, the rude hymns of the old Saxon Sternholds. They had never fought so well ; nor had the genius of their chief ever been so conspicuous. " That battle," said Napoleon, " was a masterpiece. Of itself it is sufficient to entitle Frederic to a place in the first rank among generals." The victory was complete. Twenty-seven thousand Austrians were killed, wounded, or taken ; fifty stand of colors, a hundred guns, four thousand wagons, fell into the hands of the Prussians. Breslau opened its gates ; Silesia was reconquered ; Charles of Loraine retired to hide his shame and sorrow at Brussels ; and Frederic allowed his troops to take some repose in winter quarters, after a campaign, to the vicissitudes of which it will be difficult to find any parallel in ancient or modern history.

---

22. **Old Saxon Sternholds.** Thomas Sternhold (birth uncertain–1549), an old English writer, who translated the Psalms into metrical English for church use. Macaulay means here the ancient chants, which had been prepared by Saxon monks for the people to sing.

The King's fame filled all the world. He had, during the last year, maintained a contest, on terms of advantage, against three powers, the weakest of which had more than three times his resources. He had fought four great pitched battles against superior forces. Three of these battles he had 5 gained; and the defeat of Kolin, repaired as it had been, rather raised than lowered his military renown. The victory of Leuthen is, to this day, the proudest on the roll of Prussian fame. Leipsic indeed, and Waterloo, produced consequences more important to mankind. But the glory of Leipsic must be 10 shared by the Prussians with the Austrians and Russians; and at Waterloo the British infantry bore the burden and heat of the day. The victory of Rosbach was, in a military point of view, less honorable than that of Leuthen; for it was gained over an incapable general and a disorganized army; but the 15 moral effect which it produced was immense. All the preceding triumphs of Frederic had been triumphs over Germans, and could excite no emotions of national pride among the German people. It was impossible that a Hessian or a Hanoverian could feel any patriotic exultation at hearing that 20 Pomeranians had slaughtered Moravians, or that Saxon banners had been hung in the churches of Berlin. Indeed, though the military character of the Germans justly stood high throughout the world, they could boast of no great day which belonged to them as a people; of no Agincourt, of no 25 Bannockburn. Most of their victories had been gained over each other; and their most splendid exploits against foreigners had been achieved under the command of Eugene, who was himself a foreigner. The news of the battle of Rosbach stirred the blood of the whole of the mighty population from the Alps 30 to the Baltic, and from the borders of Courland to those of

---

9. **Leipsig.** In 1813 Napoleon received a crushing defeat at the battle of Leipsig. This was called the "battle of the nations."

9. **Waterloo.** Napoleon was defeated at the battle of Waterloo, near Brussels, in Belgium, June 18, 1815, by the allied armies of Europe.

25. **Agincourt.** At the battle of Agincourt, in 1415, Henry V. of England defeated a vastly superior French army.

26. **Bannockburn.** Edward II. of England with an army of 100,000 men was totally defeated by 30,000 Scotchmen under Robert Bruce.

Loraine.   Westphalia and Lower Saxony had been deluged by
a great host of strangers, whose speech was unintelligible, and
whose petulant and licentious manners had excited the strongest feelings of disgust and hatred.   That great host had been
5 put to flight by a small band of German warriors, led by a
prince of German blood on the side of father and mother, and
marked by the fair hair and the clear blue eye of Germany.
Never since the dissolution of the empire of Charlemagne
had the Teutonic race won such a field against the French.
10 The tidings called forth a general burst of delight and pride
from the whole of the great family which spoke the various
dialects of the ancient language of Arminius.   The fame of
Frederic began to supply, in some degree, the place of a common government and of a common capital.   It became a rally-
15 ing-point for all true Germans, a subject of mutual congratula-
tion to the Bavarian and the Westphalian, to the citizen of
Frankfort and the citizen of Nuremburg.   Then first it was
manifest that the Germans were truly a nation.   Then first was
discernible that patriotic spirit which, in 1813, achieved the
20 great deliverance of central Europe, and which still guards,
and long will guard, against foreign ambition the old freedom
of the Rhine.

Nor were the effects produced by that celebrated day merely
political.   The greatest masters of German poetry and elo-
25 quence have admitted that, though the great King neither
valued nor understood his native language, though he looked
on France as the only seat of taste and philosophy, yet, in his
own despite, he did much to emancipate the genius of his
countrymen from the foreign yoke ; and that, in the act of
30 vanquishing Soubise, he was, unintentionally, rousing the
spirit which soon began to question the literary precedence of

---

8. **Empire of Charlemagne.** The Empire of Charlemagne extended
from the river Ebro in Spain to the Elbe in Northern Germany, a distance
of almost a thousand miles.

12. **Arminius.** An ancient German hero, born in 16 B.C. He entered the
Roman army and obtained some fame as a soldier.   In 9 A.D., indignant at
the wrongs of his countrymen, he persuaded a Roman army to cross the
Rhine, where, entangled in the marshes and forests, they were easily
defeated by the Germans.

20. **Deliverance of Central Europe.** At the battle of Leipsig.

Boileau and Voltaire. So strangely do events confound all
the plans of man. A prince who read only French, who wrote
only French, who aspired to rank as a French classic, became,
quite unconsciously, the means of liberating half the Continent from the dominion of that French criticism of which he [5]
was himself, to the end of his life, a slave. Yet even the enthusiasm of Germany in favor of Frederic hardly equaled the
enthusiasm of England. The birthday of our ally was celebrated with as much enthusiasm as that of our own sovereign ;
and at night the streets of London were in a blaze with illum- [10]
inations. Portraits of the Hero of Rosbach, with his cocked
hat and long pigtail, were in every house. An attentive ob-
server will, at this day, find in the parlors of old-fashioned
inns, and in the portfolios of printsellers, twenty portraits of
Frederic for one of George II. The sign-painters were every- [15]
where employed in touching up Admiral Vernon into the King
of Prussia. This enthusiasm was strong among religious
people, and especially among the Methodists, who knew that
the French and Austrians were Papists, and supposed Frederic
to be the Joshua or Gideon of the Reformed faith. One of [20]
Whitfield's hearers, on the day on which thanks for the battle
of Leuthen were returned at the Tabernacle, made the following exquisitely ludicrous entry in a diary, part of which has
come down to us : " The Lord stirred up the King of Prussia
and his soldiers to pray. They kept three fast days, and spent [25]
about an hour praying and singing psalms before they engaged
the enemy. O ! how good it is to pray and fight ! " Some

---

1. **Nicolas Boileau** (1636–1711). An eminent French poet and satirist.
Boileau is the analogue of Pope in French literature. Among his best
works are *The Reading Desk* (" Le Lutrin ") and *The Art of Poetry* (" L'Art
poétique ").
16. **Edward Vernon** (1684–1757). A popular English naval hero. In
1739 he took Porto Bello from the Spaniards with only six ships. In the
last century all the country inns had a swinging sign over the door, generally
bearing the portrait either of the king or of some popular hero.
21. **George Whitfield** (1714–1770). An eminent English preacher, and
founder of the sect of Calvinistic Methodists. " Hume pronounced him,"
says Robert Southey, " the most vigorous preacher he had ever heard, and
said it was worth while to go twenty miles to hear him. But perhaps the
greatest proof of his persuasive powers was when he drew from Benjamin
Franklin's pocket the money which that clear, cool reasoner had determined
not to give." See Franklin's own account of this as given in his intensely
interesting autobiography.

young Englishmen of rank proposed to visit Germany as volunteers, for the purpose of learning the art of war under the greatest of commanders. This last proof of British attachment and admiration, Frederic politely but firmly declined.
5 His camp was no place for amateur students of military science. The Prussian discipline was rigorous even to cruelty. The officers, while in the field, were expected to practice an abstemiousness and self-denial such as was hardly surpassed by the most rigid monastic orders. However noble their birth,
10 however high their rank in the service, they were not permitted to eat from anything better than pewter. It was a high crime even in a count and field-marshal to have a single silver spoon among his baggage. Gay young Englishmen of twenty thousand a year, accustomed to liberty and to luxury,
15 would not easily submit to these Spartan restraints. The King could not venture to keep them in order as he kept his own subjects in order. Situated as he was with respect to England, he could not well imprison or shoot refractory Howards and Cavendishes. On the other hand, the example of a
20 few fine gentlemen, attended by chariots and livery servants, eating in plate, and drinking Champagne and Tokay, was enough to corrupt his whole army. He thought it best to make a stand at first, and civilly refused to admit such dangerous companions among his troops.

25 The help of England was bestowed in a manner far more useful and more acceptable. An annual subsidy of near seven hundred thousand pounds enabled the King to add probably more than fifty thousand men to his army. Pitt, now at the height of power and popularity, undertook the task of defend-
30 ing Western Germany against France, and asked Frederic only for the loan of a general. The general selected was Prince Ferdinand of Brunswick, who had attained high distinction in

---

19. **Howards and Cavendishes.** Two of the greatest English noble families.
28. **William Pitt, Earl of Chatham** (1708–1778). One of the greatest statesmen England has ever seen. As prime minister he governed England with singular wisdom and firmness. To Americans William Pitt is of special interest, because of the strong opposition he exercised against the coercive measures passed by parliament in the beginning of our Revolution.

the Prussian service. He was put at the head of an army, partly English, partly Hanoverian, partly composed of mercenaries hired from the petty princes of the empire. He soon vindicated the choice of the two allied courts, and proved himself the second general of the age. 5

Frederic passed the winter at Breslau, in reading, writing, and preparing for the next campaign. The havoc which the war had made among his troops was rapidly repaired ; and in the spring of 1758 he was again ready for the conflict. Prince Ferdinand kept the French in check. The King in the mean 10 time, after attempting against the Austrians some operations which led to no very important result, marched to encounter the Russians, who, slaying, burning, and wasting wherever they turned, had penetrated into the heart of his realm. He gave them battle at Zorndorf, near Frankfort on the Oder. 15 The fight was long and bloody. Quarter was neither given nor taken ; for the Germans and Scythians regarded each other with bitter aversion, and the sight of the ravages committed by the half-savage invaders had incensed the King and his army. The Russians were overthrown with great slaughter ; 20 and for a few months no further danger was to be apprehended from the east.

A day of thanksgiving was proclaimed by the King, and was celebrated with pride and delight by his people. The rejoicings in England were not less enthusiastic or less sincere. 25 This may be selected as the point of time at which the military glory of Frederic reached the zenith. In the short space of three quarters of a year he had won three great battles over the armies of three mighty and warlike monarchies, France, Austria, and Russia. 30

But it was decreed that the temper of that strong mind should be tried by both extremes of fortune in rapid succession. Close upon this series of triumphs came a series of disasters, such as would have blighted the fame and broken the heart of almost any other commander. Yet Frederic, in the 35 midst of his calamities, was still an object of admiration to his subjects, his allies, and his enemies. Overwhelmed by adversity, sick of life, he still maintained the contest, greater in defeat, in flight, and in what seemed hopeless ruin, than on the fields of his proudest victories.

Having vanquished the Russians, he hastened into Saxony
5 to oppose the troops of the Empress Queen, commanded by Daun, the most cautious, and Laudohn, the most inventive and enterprising of her generals. These two celebrated commanders agreed on a scheme, in which the prudence of the one and the vigor of the other seem to have been happily com-
10 bined. At dead of night they surprised the King in his camp at Hochkirchen. His presence of mind saved his troops from destruction ; but nothing could save them from defeat and severe loss. Marshal Keith was among the slain. The first roar of the guns roused the noble exile from his rest, and he
15 was instantly in the front of the battle. He received a dangerous wound, but refused to quit the field, and was in the act of rallying his broken troops, when an Austrian bullet terminated his checkered and eventful life.

The misfortune was serious. But of all generals Frederic
20 understood best how to repair defeat, and Daun understood least how to improve victory. In a few days the Prussian army was as formidable as before the battle. The prospect was, however, gloomy. An Austrian army under General Harsch had invaded Silesia, and invested the fortress of Neisse.
25 Daun, after his success at Hochkirchen, had written to Harsch in very confident terms : "Go on with your operations against Neisse. Be quite at ease as to the King. I will give a good account of him." In truth, the position of the Prussians was full of difficulties. Between them and Silesia lay
30 the victorious army of Daun. It was not easy for them to reach Silesia at all. If they did reach it, they left Saxony exposed to the Austrians. But the vigor and activity of Frederic surmounted every obstacle. He made a circuitous march of extraordinary rapidity, passed Daun, hastened into

---

13. **James Keith** (1696–1758). A Scotch nobleman, exiled from England for political reasons. Both he and his brother were great favorites of Frederic.

Silesia, raised the siege of Neisse, and drove Harsch into Bohemia. Daun availed himself of the King's absence to attack Dresden. The Prussians defended it desperately. The inhabitants of that wealthy and polished capital begged in vain for mercy from the garrison within, and from the besieg- 5 ers without. The beautiful suburbs were burned to the ground. It was clear that the town, if won at all, would be won street by street by the bayonet. At this conjuncture came news, that Frederic, having cleared Silesia of his enemies, was returning by forced marches into Saxony. Daun retired from 10 before Dresden, and fell back into the Austrian territories. The King, over heaps of ruins, made his triumphant entry into the unhappy metropolis, which had so cruelly expiated the weak and perfidious policy of its sovereign. It was now the 20th of November. The cold weather suspended military 15 operations ; and the King again took up his winter quarters at Breslau.

The third of the seven terrible years was over ; and Frederic still stood his ground. He had been recently tried by domestic as well as by military disasters. On the 14th of October, 20 the day on which he was defeated at Hochkirchen, the day on the anniversary of which, forty-eight years later, a defeat far more tremendous laid the Prussian monarchy in the dust, died Wilhelmina, Margravine of Bareuth. From the accounts which we have of her, by her own hand, and by the hands of 25 the most discerning of her contemporaries, we should pronounce her to have been coarse, indelicate, and a good hater, but not destitute of kind and generous feelings. Her mind, naturally strong and observant, had been highly cultivated ; and she was, and deserved to be, Frederic's favorite sister. 30 He felt the loss as much as it was in his iron nature to feel the loss of anything but a province or a battle.

At Breslau, during the winter, he was indefatigable in his poetical labors. The most spirited lines, perhaps, that he

---

22. **A defeat.** On May 14, 1806, the Prussians were completely defeated by Napoleon in the double battle of Jena and Auerstädt. Napoleon marched to Berlin and entered it October 27th.

ever wrote, are to be found in a bitter lampoon on Lewis and
Madame de Pompadour, which he composed at this time, and
sent to Voltaire. The verses were, indeed, so good that Voltaire was afraid that he might himself be suspected of having
5 written them, or at least of having corrected them; and
partly from fright, partly, we fear, from love of mischief, sent
them to the Duke of Choiseul, then prime minister of France.
Choiseul very wisely determined to encounter Frederic at
Frederic's own weapons, and applied for assistance to Palissot,
10 who had some skill as a versifier, and some little talent for
satire. Palissot produced some very stinging lines on the
moral and literary character of Frederic, and these lines the
Duke sent to Voltaire. This war of couplets, following close
on the carnage of Zorndorf and the conflagration of Dresden,
15 illustrates well the strangely compounded character of the
King of Prussia.

At this moment he was assailed by a new enemy. Benedict
XIV., the best and wisest of the two hundred and fifty successors of St. Peter, was no more. During the short interval
20 between his reign and that of his disciple Ganganelli, the
chief seat in the Church of Rome was filled by Rezzonico, who
took the name of Clement XIII. This absurd priest determined to try what the weight of his authority could effect in
favor of the orthodox Maria Theresa against a heretic king.
25 At the high mass on Christmas-day, a sword with a rich belt
and scabbard, a hat of crimson velvet lined with ermine, and
a dove of pearls, the mystic symbol of the Divine Comforter,
were solemnly blessed by the supreme pontiff, and were sent
with great ceremony to Marshal Daun, the conqueror of Kolin
30 and Hochkirchen. This mark of favor had more than once
been bestowed by the Popes on the great champions of the
faith. Similar honors had been paid, more than six centuries
earlier, by Urban II. to Godfrey of Bouillon. Similar honors

20. **Ganganelli** (1705–1774). An Italian cardinal, who became Pope under
the title of Clement XIV. He took prompt measures to conciliate the
various foreign courts which his predecessor had offended.

33. **Godfrey of Bouillon** (1058–1100). The illustrious leader of the first
crusade. He took Jerusalem in 1099, and by the unanimous wish of the crusa-
ders was chosen king of the conquered city, but refused the title of royalty,

had been conferred on Alba for destroying the liberties of the
Low Countries, and on John Sobiesky after the deliverance of
Vienna.   But the presents which were received with profound
reverence by the Baron of the Holy Sepulcher in the eleventh
century, and which had not wholly lost their value even in the 5
seventeenth century, appeared inexpressibly ridiculous to a
generation which read Montesquieu and Voltaire.   Frederic
wrote sarcastic verses on the gifts, the giver, and the receiver.
But the public wanted no prompter ; and a universal roar of
laughter from Petersburg to Lisbon reminded the Vatican that 10
the age of crusades was over.

The fourth campaign, the most disastrous of all the cam
paigns of this fearful war, had now opened.   The Austrians
filled Saxony and menaced Berlin.   The Russians defeated the
King's generals on the Oder, threatened Silesia, effected a 15
junction with Laudohn, and intrenched themselves strongly at
Kunersdorf.   Frederic hastened to attack them.   A great battle was fought.   During the earlier part of the day everything yielded to the impetuosity of the Prussians, and to the
skill of their chief.   The lines were forced.   Half the Russian 20
guns were taken.   The King sent off a courier to Berlin with
two lines, announcing a complete victory.   But, in the mean
time, the stubborn Russians, defeated yet unbroken, had
taken up their stand in an almost impregnable position, on
an eminence where the Jews of Frankfort were wont to bury 25

---

saying, " he would never accept a crown of gold in a city where his Saviour
had worn a crown of thorns."   Godfrey is the hero of Tasso's great Italian
epic, " Jerusalem Delivered;" and the poet appears not to have exaggerated
the merits of a character which was a rare combination of wisdom and
heroism, with Christian virtues of a high order.
  1. **Ferdinando, Duke of Alba** (1508–1582).   A celebrated Spanish
general under Charles V.   In 1567 he quelled an insurrection of the Protestants in the Low Countries; but such was the cruelty with which he treated
any suspected heretics, that historians have said that his brutality was the
principal reason why Spain lost the Low Countries.   Alba was accustomed
to boast that in the space of four years he had brought no fewer than
eighteen thousand persons to the scaffold.
  2. **John Sobiesky** (1629–1696).   A famous Polish warrior and king.
Many times he saved his country from Turkish invasions.   In 1683 he
marched with a Polish army to the aid of the Austrians, who were besieged
in Vienna by a great Turkish army, and with the help of his German and
French allies expelled the Turks from the country.   He was revered in
Poland as the savior of his country.
  4. **Baron of the Holy Sepulcher.**   Godfrey de Bouillon.   This title
was a crusading order of knighthood.

their dead. Here the battle recommenced. The Prussian infantry, exhausted by six hours of hard fighting under a sun which equaled the tropical heat, were yet brought up repeatly to the attack, but in vain. The King led three charges in
5 person. Two horses were killed under him. The officers of his staff fell all round him. His coat was pierced by several bullets. All was in vain. His infantry was driven back with frightful slaughter. Terror began to spread fast from man to man. At that moment, the fiery cavalry of Laudohn, still
10 fresh, rushed on the wavering ranks. Then followed a universal rout. Frederic himself was on the point of falling into the hands of the conquerors, and was with difficulty saved by a gallant officer, who, at the head of a handful of hussars, made good a diversion of a few minutes. Shattered in body,
15 shattered in mind, the King reached that night a village which the Cossacks had plundered; and there, in a ruined and deserted farm-house, flung himself on a heap of straw. He had sent to Berlin a second despatch very different from his first: " Let the royal family leave Berlin. Send the Archives to
20 Potsdam. The town may make terms with the enemy."

The defeat was, in truth, overwhelming. Of fifty thousand men who had that morning marched under the black eagles, not three thousand remained together. The King bethought him again of his corrosive sublimate, and wrote to bid adieu
25 to his friends, and to give directions as to the measures to be taken in the event of his death: " I have no resource left "— such is the language of one of his letters—" all is lost. I will not survive the ruin of my country. Farewell forever."

But the mutual jealousies of the confederates prevented them
30 from following up their victory. They lost a few days in loitering and squabbling; and a few days, improved by Frederic, were worth more than the years of other men. On the morning after the battle, he had got together eighteen thousand of his troops. Very soon his force amounted to thirty thousand.
35 Guns were procured from the neighboring fortresses; and

---

22. **Black Eagles.** The national emblem of Prussia.

there was again an army. Berlin was for the present safe;
but calamities came pouring on the King in uninterrupted succession. One of his generals, with a large body of troops, was
taken at Maxen ; another was defeated at Meissen ; and when
at length the campaign of 1759 closed, in the midst of a rigor- 5
ous winter, the situation of Prussia appeared desperate. The
only consoling circumstance was, that, in the West, Ferdinand
of Brunswick had been more fortunate than his master ; and
by a series of exploits, of which the battle of Minden was the
most glorious, had removed all apprehension of danger on the 10
side of France.

The fifth year was now about to commence. It seemed impossible that the Prussian territories, repeatedly devastated by
hundreds of thousands of invaders, could longer support the
contest. But the King carried on war as no European power 15
has ever carried on war, except the Committee of Public Safety
during the great agony of the French Revolution. He governed his kingdom as he would have governed a besieged town,
not caring to what extent property was destroyed, or the pur-
suits of civil life suspended, so that he did but make head 20
against the enemy. As long as there was a man left in
Prussia, that man might carry a musket ; as long as there was
a horse left, that horse might draw artillery. The coin was
debased, the civil functionaries were left unpaid ; in some
provinces civil government altogether ceased to exist. But 25
there were still rye bread and potatoes ; there were still lead
and gunpowder ; and, while the means of sustaining and destroying life remained, Frederic was determined to fight it out
to the very last.

The earlier part of the campaign of 1760 was unfavorable to 30
him. Berlin was again occupied by the enemy. Great contributions were levied on the inhabitants, and the royal palace
was plundered. But at length, after two years of calamity,
victory came back to his arms. At Lignitz he gained a great

---

16. **Committee of Public Safety.** During the French Revolution,
from April, 1793, France was governed by a committee composed of about
ten men. This small body of men was entrusted with absolutely unlimited
power to govern France as was necessary to the success of the Revolution.

battle over Laudohn ; at Torgau, after a day of horrible carnage, he triumphed over Daun. The fifth year closed, and still
the event was in suspense. In the countries where the war
had raged, the misery and exhaustion were more appalling
5 than ever ; but still there were left men and beasts, arms and
food, and still Frederic fought on. In truth he had now been
baited into savageness. His heart was ulcerated with hatred.
The implacable resentment with which his enemies persecuted
him, though originally provoked by his own unprincipled am-
10 bition, excited in him a thirst for vengeance which he did not
even attempt to conceal. " It is hard," he says in one of his
letters, " for man to bear what I bear. I begin to feel that,
as the Italians say, revenge is a pleasure for the gods. My
philosophy is worn out by suffering. I am no saint, like those
15 of whom we read in the legends ; and I will own that I should
die content if only I could first inflict a portion of the misery
which I endure."

Borne up by such feelings, he struggled with various success,
but constant glory, through the campaign of 1761. On the
20 whole, the result of this campaign was disastrous to Prussia.
No great battle was gained by the enemy ; but, in spite of the
desperate bounds of the hunted tiger, the circle of pursuers
was fast closing round him. Laudohn had surprised the important fortress of Schweidnitz. With that fortress, half of
25 Silesia, and the command of the most important defiles
through the mountains, had been transferred to the Austrians.
The Russians had overpowered the King's generals in Pomerania. The country was so completely desolated that he began, by his own confession, to look round him with blank
30 despair, unable to imagine where recruits, horses, or provisions
were to be found.

Just at this time two great events brought on a complete
change in the relations of almost all the powers of Europe.
One of those events was the retirement of Mr. Pitt from office :
35 the other was the death of the Empress Elizabeth of Russia.

The retirement of Pitt seemed to be an omen of utter ruin
to the House of Brandenburg. His proud and vehement

nature was incapable of anything that looked like either fear
or treachery. He had often declared that, while he was in
power, England should never make a peace of Utrecht, should
never, for any selfish object, abandon an ally even in the last
extremity of distress. The Continental war was his own war. 5
He had been bold enough, he who in former times had attacked, with irresistible powers of oratory, the Hanoverian
policy of Carteret, and the German subsidies of Newcastle, to
declare that Hanover ought to be as dear to us as Hampshire,
and that he would conquer America in Germany. He had 10
fallen ; and the power which he had exercised, not always with
discretion, but always with vigor and genius, had devolved on
a favorite who was the representative of the Tory party, of the
party which had thwarted William, which had persecuted Marlborough, and which had given up the Catalans to the ven- 15
geance of Philip of Anjou. To make peace with France, to shake
off, with all, or more than all, the speed compatible with
decency, every Continental connection, these were among the
chief objects of the new Minister. The policy then followed
inspired Frederic with an unjust, but deep and bitter aversion 20
to the English name, and produced effects which are still felt
throughout the civilized world. To that policy it was owing
that, some years later, England could not find on the whole
Continent a single ally to stand by her, in her extreme need,
against the House of Bourbon. To that policy it was owing 25
that Frederic, alienated from England, was compelled to con-
nect himself closely, during his later years, with Russia, and

3. **Peace of Utrecht.** By this peace in 1713 Great Britain withdrew
from the so-called " grand alliance " against France at the end of the War of
the Spanish Succession.
8. **Thomas Pelham, Duke of Newcastle** (1693-1768). A famous
Whig minister of state. He was considered by his contemporaries a " dunce,
a driveler, a child who never knew his own mind, but he overreached them
all around," says Macaulay. He was a man with a passionate love of power,
and a perfect indifference as to whether he got it by fair means or foul.
16. **Philip of Anjou.** From 1701 until 1714 all Europe was in arms,
owing to the dispute about the succession to the Spanish crown. Louis XIV.
of France gave the crown to his grandson Philip of Anjou, while the rest of
Europe thought that Austria ought to have it. By the Peace of Utrecht in
1713 Philip of Anjou was confirmed in his possessions, among which was
Catalonia, the inhabitants of which province had opposed most bitterly his
succession to the crown.

was induced to assist in that great crime, the fruitful parent
of other great crimes, the first partition of Poland.

Scarcely had the retreat of Mr. Pitt deprived Prussia of her
only friend, when the death of Elizabeth produced an entire
5 revolution in the politics of the North. The Grand Duke
Peter, her nephew, who now ascended the Russian throne, was
not merely free from the prejudices which his aunt had entertained against Frederic, but was a worshiper, a servile imi-
tator of the great King. The days of the new Czar's govern-
10 ment were few and evil, but sufficient to produce a change in
the whole state of Christendom. He set the Prussian prisoners
at liberty, fitted them out decently, and sent them back to
their master ; he withdrew his troops from the provinces which
Elizabeth had decided on incorporating with her dominions ;
15 and he absolved all those Prussian subjects, who had been
compelled to swear fealty to Russia, from their engagements.

Not content with concluding peace on terms favorable to
Prussia, he solicited rank in the Prussian service, dressed himself in a Prussian uniform, wore the Black Eagle of Prussia on
20 his breast, made preparations for visiting Prussia, in order to
have an interview with the object of his idolatry, and actually
sent fifteen thousand excellent troops to reinforce the shattered
army of Frederic. Thus strengthened, the King speedily repaired the losses of the preceding year, reconquered Silesia,
25 defeated Daun at Buckersdorf, invested and retook Schweidnitz, and, at the close of the year, presented to the forces of
Maria Theresa a front as formidable as before the great reverses of 1759. Before the end of the campaign, his friend
the Emperor Peter, having, by a series of absurd insults to the
30 institutions, manners, and feelings of his people, united them
in hostility to his person and government, was deposed and
murdered. The Empress, who, under the title of Catherine
the Second, now assumed the supreme power, was, at the commencement of her administration, by no means partial to
35 Frederic, and refused to permit her troops to remain under his
command. But she observed the peace made by her husband ;

and Prussia was no longer threatened by danger from the East.

England and France at the same time paired off together. They concluded a treaty, by which they bound themselves to observe neutrality with respect to the German war. Thus the 5 coalitions on both sides were dissolved ; and the original enemies, Austria and Prussia, remained alone confronting each other.

Austria had undoubtedly far greater means than Prussia, and was less exhausted by hostilities ; yet it seemed hardly 10 possible that Austria could effect alone what she had in vain attempted to effect when supported by France on the one side, and by Russia on the other. Danger also began to menace the Imperial house from another quarter. The Ottoman Porte held threatening language, and a hundred thousand Turks 15 were mustered on the frontiers of Hungary. The proud and revengeful spirit of the Empress Queen at length gave way ; and, in February, 1763, the peace of Hubertsburg put an end to the conflict which had, during seven years, devastated Germany. The King ceded nothing. The whole Continent in 20 arms had proved unable to tear Silesia from that iron grasp.

The war was over. Frederic was safe. His glory was beyond the reach of envy. If he had not made conquests as vast as those of Alexander, of Cæsar, and of Napoleon, if he had not, on fields of battle, enjoyed the constant success of 25 Marlborough and Wellington, he had yet given an example unrivaled in history of what capacity and resolution can effect against the greatest superiority of power and the utmost spite of fortune. He entered Berlin in triumph, after an absence of more than six years. The streets were brilliantly lighted 30 up, and, as he passed along in an open carriage, with Ferdinand of Brunswick at his side, the multitude saluted him with loud praises and blessings. He was moved by those marks of attachment, and repeatedly exclaimed, "Long live my dear people ! Long live my children !" Yet, even in the midst of 35 that gay spectacle, he could not but perceive everywhere the traces of destruction and decay. The city had been more

than once plundered. The population had considerably dimin-
ished. Berlin, however, had suffered little when compared
with most parts of the kingdom. The ruin of private fortunes,
the distress of all ranks, was such as might appall the firmest
5 mind. Almost every province had been the seat of war, and of
war conducted with merciless ferocity. Clouds of Croatians had
descended on Silesia. Tens of thousands of Cossacks had been
let loose on Pomerania and Brandenburg. The mere contributions levied by the invaders amounted, it was said, to more
10 than a hundred millions of dollars ; and the value of what
they extorted was probably much less than the value of what
they destroyed. The fields lay uncultivated. The very seed-
corn had been devoured in the madness of hunger. Famine,
and contagious maladies produced by famine, had swept away
15 the herds and flocks ; and there was reason to fear that a
great pestilence among the human race was likely to follow in
the train of that tremendous war. Near fifteen thousand
houses had been burned to the ground. The population of the
kingdom had in seven years decreased to the frightful extent
20 of ten per cent. A sixth of the males capable of bearing arms
had actually perished on the field of battle. In some districts,
no laborers, except women, were seen in the fields at harvest-
time. In others, the traveler passed shuddering through a
succession of silent villages, in which not a single inhabitant
25 remained. The currency had been debased ; the authority of
laws and magistrates had been suspended ; the whole social
system was deranged. For, during that convulsive struggle,
everything that was not military violence was anarchy. Even
the army was disorganized. Some great generals, and a
30 crowd of excellent officers, had fallen, and it had been impossible to supply their place. The difficulty of finding recruits
had, towards the close of the war, been so great, that selection
and rejection were impossible. Whole battalions were com-
35 posed of deserters or of prisoners. It was hardly to be hoped
that thirty years of repose and industry would repair the ruin
produced by seven years of havoc. One consolatory circumstance, indeed, there was. No debt had been incurred. The

burdens of the war had been terrible, almost insupportable ; but no arrear was left to embarrass the finances in time of peace.

Here, for the present, we must pause. We have accompanied Frederic to the close of his career as a warrior. Possibly, when these Memoirs are completed, we may resume the consideration of his character, and give some account of his domestic and foreign policy, and of his private habits, during the many years of tranquillity which followed the Seven Years' War.